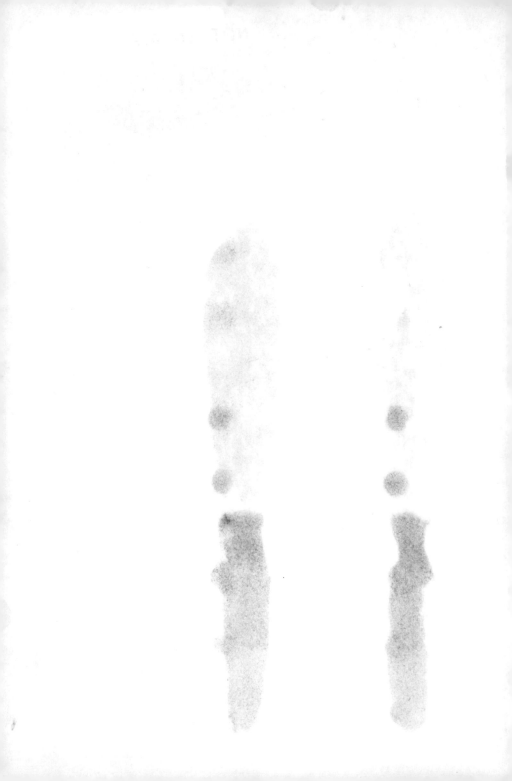

THE END
OF THE WORLD

RICHARD MORRIS studied physics at the universities of Nevada and New Mexico from 1958 to 1968, receiving his Ph.D. in 1968. Since then he has been executive director of COSMEP, an international association of little magazines and small presses which he helped to found. Morris is the author of *Light* and has published six collections of poetry and two collections of short plays with small presses. Since 1965 his poems, fiction, reviews, and essays have appeared in numerous little magazines.

THE END
OF THE WORLD

Richard Morris

ANCHOR PRESS/DOUBLEDAY
GARDEN CITY, NEW YORK
1980

The Anchor Press edition is the first publication of *The End of the World*.
It is published simultaneously in hard and paper covers.

Anchor Press edition: 1980

Library of Congress Cataloging in Publication Data

Morris, Richard, 1939–
The end of the world.
Bibliography: p. 161
Includes index.
1. Cosmology.   I. Title.
QB981.M86   523.1
ISBN 0-385-15523-9
Library of Congress Catalog Card Number 79–8437

CONTENTS

801014

PREFACE

"The end of the world" is a phrase that has several different meanings. It can be used to denote the destruction of the planet earth, the extinction of the human race or of all living creatures, or simply the end of Western civilization. In this book I have indiscriminately applied the term to all these hypothetical events —there seemed to be little point in inventing new terminology to distinguish between them. To most of us, any of these events would be "the end of the world."

I have not discussed any wildly improbable disasters, except to point out that they are unlikely. Some of the catastrophes which I describe *will* take place sooner or later. Others *may* happen, possibly before the end of this century, possibly only after a thousand years have passed. At some point, however, the events which fall in this second category will become imminent threats.

When the end of the world becomes imminent, it is not likely that there will be any technological solutions by which it can be averted. The forces of nature are more powerful than anything that man has devised, and they are likely to remain so in any foreseeable future. In fact, it may be our technology that ultimately destroys us. There already exist indications that it is rapidly getting out of control and that we must learn to proceed in a much more modest way if we are to have any hope of survival.

No sane person would suggest that we dismantle our technology and return to the Stone Age. However, it is rapidly becoming apparent that we must learn to restrain our compulsion to manipulate nature for our benefit. There are forces in the universe which could destroy us at any moment; if we provoke nature too much, they will destroy us that much sooner.

This book is not, however, an ecological treatise. If anything, it is a work of scientific popularization. In discussing the ways in which the end of the world might take place, I describe numerous discoveries which have been made in astronomy and physics during the last decade or so. I think I show that many of these do relate to the theme of the book; the more we learn about the universe, the more frightening a place it seems to be.

Long after human life comes to an end and the earth is destroyed, the universe will die also. There is currently a great deal of scientific speculation concerning the ways in which this might happen, and about whether a new universe might be born after our own comes to an end.

Some of this speculation is quite fantastic; one could go so far as to say that it is sometimes rather farfetched. Now this is no criticism; theoretical scientists have an obligation to explore the limits of knowledge, to discuss all the things that might turn out to be true. But unfortunately, works of scientific popularization all too often present such speculation as fact.

Examples of this are provided by the recent books which discuss the possibility of travel to "other universes" through black holes. While such parallel universes might exist, at present they are only an interesting theoretical possibility. At the moment we cannot even be certain that there are such things as black holes, although most scientists now believe that there are good reasons for thinking that there are.

I have, therefore, attempted to distinguish clearly between scientific fact and scientific speculation. At times the task has been difficult, for many scientific theories are currently in a state of rapid change. It is possible that some of the things which were "fact" when this book was written will have been discredited by the time it is published. I hope that the reader will forgive me if, here and there, I have hedged by discussing what science does *not* know instead of trotting out a lot of "facts."

If we knew everything, there would be no such activity as science. If the practice of science is to be described in a way that is at all accurate, one must speak of phenomena which are not understood, of theories which do not seem to quite work, of areas in which there is not yet enough experimental data to formulate any theories at all. There are quite a few references to such things in this book.

I have also tried to show how changes in theoretical outlook take place. For example, Chapter 10 contains a long discussion of the so-called steady state theory of the universe, which is now discredited. I included this in the hope that such a discussion would help to clarify the reasons why the competing big bang theory so quickly became orthodox and also to demonstrate how wrong some intuitively appealing ideas can turn out to be.

There is one additional point that I must make: some of those who read this book will note that I habitually write "he" when I mean "he or she" and use such terms as "man" in place of nonsexist alternatives such as "humanity." The reason for this is that I find many of the nonsexist terms to be awkward. They have not yet become part of our language in any natural way. Until there are some universally accepted substitutes for the old terms, I will reluctantly continue to use the latter. Any reader who objects to them should read "he or she" when I say "he," and so on.

I
THE END
OF THE WORLD

1

DRAGONS OF CHAOS

The Greek myths tell us that after Zeus had driven the Titans out of heaven, Mother Earth sought revenge for the treatment accorded her offspring by giving birth to a monster named Typhon, the largest creature ever to walk the earth. Typhon was so tall that his head knocked against the stars, his enormous wings blocked out the rays of the sun, and flaming coals flew from his mouth. A hundred black-tongued dragon heads grew from his shoulders; flames darted from their eyes. Strange sounds came from these heads. Sometimes it was speech that the gods could easily understand, and sometimes it resembled the bellowing of enraged bulls. At one moment the heads would roar like lions; at the next they would yelp like puppies.

When the gods saw Typhon advancing toward Olympus, they fled in dismay to Egypt where they attempted to hide by changing themselves into animals. Zeus became a ram, Apollo a crow, Dionysus a goat. Hera transformed herself into a cow, while Aphrodite became a fish and Ares a boar.

Of all the gods, only Athena possessed the courage to retain her true form.

Berated by Athena for his cowardice, Zeus at last resolved to do battle with the monster. Throwing a thunderbolt at Typhon, he advanced upon the horrible creature, swinging the sickle that he had used to castrate his grandfather Uranus. But when the two grappled, Typhon easily disarmed Zeus and used his weapon to remove the sinews of the god's hands and feet. Then he dragged the helpless god to the Corycian Cave. There the immortal Zeus lay, unable to move, while Delphyne, Typhon's serpent-tailed sister monster, stood guard.

It appeared that all was lost. Now that the champion of the gods had fallen, it seemed that the end of the world was imminent, that Typhon and the forces of chaos would quickly overwhelm the remaining deities, crushing any resistance that they might offer with ease. In order to stave off the coming disaster, Hermes and Pan resorted to a ruse. They went secretly to the cave where Zeus lay captive, and after Pan had frightened off Delphyne by making a terrible noise, Hermes, the physician and god of thieves, discovered where the sinews had been hidden and replaced them in Zeus's limbs.

Zeus returned at once to Olympus. Mounting a chariot drawn by winged horses, he did battle with Typhon once again. Typhon picked up entire mountains, hurling them at Zeus, but the god used his thunderbolts to make the mountains rebound. Typhon fled, and Zeus pursued him.

It is not clear what happened next. We only know that Zeus found a way to imprison his antagonist, who was also immortal and who therefore could not be killed. Some say that Zeus hurled Mount Aetna upon the creature and that Typhon still lives beneath it, belching fire to this day. According to Hesiod, however, Zeus hurled Typhon down into Tartarus. There, Hesiod says, Typhon remains, as malevolent as ever. Lying in Tartarus, he fashions the fierce winds that whip up storms at sea, scattering ships and killing sailors, and bringing death and destruction to the coastal lands.

That Typhon was as immortal as the gods is significant. Although the myths make no explicit mention of the fact, there seems to be an implication to the effect that, given the opportunity, Typhon might free himself and again threaten the world with destruction. Imprisoned as he is, he is still able, depending upon the version of the myth that one follows, to wreak destruction either by causing volcanic eruptions or by creating storms and hurricanes. Although Typhon can be subdued, he cannot be destroyed; the destructive forces of nature, which Typhon symbolizes, are too powerful to ever be wholly eliminated.

The gods of Greek mythology are generally personifications either of human activities or of natural phenomena. Ares is the god of war, Aphrodite the goddess of love, and Poseidon the god of the oceans. There are gods or goddesses which represent the sun, the moon, the earth, the harvest, and fertility. There is a god for every river, and a god for each of the four winds. There is a god of sleep, a goddess of the dawn, a goddess of the hunt, and a goddess of the night.

To men and women of traditional societies, nature is no abstract entity, it is a living, breathing thing. Nature is peopled with supernatural but anthropomorphic beings. Phenomena can be conceived, endowed with human traits, and made into gods or goddesses, demigods or monsters. Typhon is no exception. He is more than a terrifying being who gives the Olympians a lot of trouble; he is the personification of the forces of chaos, which the gods must hold at bay if heaven and earth are not to be destroyed.

Monsters of chaos are found in virtually every ancient mythology. More often than not, chaos is symbolized by a dragon, serpent, or sea monster which the chief god must overcome. The ancient Vedic hymns of India sing, again and again, of a battle between Indra, king of the gods, and the monstrous dragon Vritra. In Japanese mythology, the god Susano-o must overcome an eight-headed serpent. The Egyptian god Re (or Ra) does combat with the dragon Apophis. The Nahuatl gods Quetzalcoatl and Tezcatlipoca must vanquish a thing with countless mouths that swims in the formless primeval waters. Only in China do dragons seem to be benign.

The ancient cultures of the Middle East provide us with an entire group of related myths about a battle between a chief god and the chaos dragon. In Assyro-Babylonian mythology, the story of the conquest of the dragon is combined with a creation myth. After the god Marduk kills the monster Tiamat, a symbol of the chaos that existed before the world was formed, he cuts her (in the Middle East the dragon is frequently thought of as being female) in half, using one part of the corpse to fashion the heavens and the other to make the earth.

One would think that this would imply, at least in Assyro-Babylonian mythology, that chaos had once and for all been conquered. This does not seem to be the case, however. As Mircea Eliade has pointed out in *The Myth of the Eternal Return*, there was a sense in which the combat was an endless one. Marduk had to slay Tiamat all over again at the beginning of every new year in order to renew the earth.

Variations of the Tiamat myth are found in other Middle Eastern mythologies. In Canaanite myth, the god Baal must slay the seven-headed dragon Lotan. In the Old Testament, Lotan becomes the sea monster Leviathan, the antagonist of Yahweh. The Old Testament is not very consistent in naming the chaos dragon, however. In Isaiah 51:9–11 it is called Rahab, and Genesis contains a reference to Tiamat herself— the Hebrew word for "the deep," *tehom*, used in Genesis 1:2 to describe the original watery chaos, is thought to be a corruption of the name Tiamat. Since Tiamat is sometimes described as a sea monster who presided over the formless primeval waters, it is not unlikely that it is she who is being named here. Biblical scholars have, incidentally, noted other similarities between the biblical account of the creation of the firmament and the Assyro-Babylonian creation story.

In the New Testament the dragon of chaos is identified with Satan. In Revelation 12:7–9, we read:

> And there was war in heaven: Michael and his angels fought against the dragon; and the dragon fought and his angels,
> And prevailed not; neither was their place found any more in heaven.
> And the great dragon was cast out, that old serpent, called the Devil, and Satan, which deceiveth the whole world: he was cast out into the earth, and his angels were cast out with him.

In medieval times the chaos dragon underwent various metamorphoses, appearing, among other forms, in the guise of the Antichrist. Yet he remained a symbol of the destruction that threatened the end of the world.

Medieval thought produced complex apocalypses constructed from passages in Revelation and from various prophecies in the Old and New Testaments. It was believed that, immediately before the Second Coming, cataclysmic events would take place and that the Antichrist would appear to lead the forces of chaos. He would summon the demonic hosts of Gog and Magog to do battle with the followers of Christ at a place called Armageddon. At the end of the battle, God would send lightning down from heaven, annihilating Satan, the Antichrist, and their followers. But, even in defeat, the forces of chaos would have brought about the end of the world, for when the battle was over, the Last Judgment would begin.

In Scandinavian mythology, on the other hand, chaos is to be victorious. The gods are fated to be destroyed at Ragnarok. Odin will be swallowed by the great wolf Fenrir, and Thor will perish in a battle with his old nemesis the Midgard

serpent. As the gods and the monsters kill one another,
heaven and earth will catch fire, bringing the world to an
end.

After the passage of an indefinite period of time, a new
earth will be created and life will begin again. Although the
myths are silent on this point, it is easy to guess that the new
world is destined to have chaos monsters of its own, for in
every mythology the battle with chaos is one that goes on for
as long as the world endures. It is difficult to discover a set of
myths in which the world is not threatened by the destructive forces of nature in one guise or another. The ancient
peoples who made up all these stories in order to explain
their perceptions of the world knew how fearsome nature
could be.

The contrast between our outlook and that of the ancient
myths is striking. Blinded by our technological hubris, we no
longer have any great fear of the destructive powers of nature. Pretending that the dragons of chaos do not exist, we
complacently treat the natural environment as something to
be manipulated for our own benefit. Grown smug after a few
hundred years of technological achievement, we disdain to
fear the malevolent aspects of nature. We often think of hurricanes and floods as annoyances which cause property damage, not as threats to our lives. We no longer believe that
there may be forces in the universe which will eventually destroy us.

Not content with exterminating other species of life by destroying their habitats, we engage in activities that threaten
our own survival. We make over forest land, thereby changing climatic patterns. We have increased our numbers to
such an extent that we are perpetually in danger of outgrow-
ing our food supplies. We continue to pollute our rivers and
oceans, and the atmosphere as well, the latter to such an extent that many scientists are now afraid that the protective
ozone layer is being destroyed. We stockpile nuclear weapons

and contaminate the earth with radioactive wastes from our reactors. We engage in potentially dangerous genetic research, while admitting that our knowledge in this area is so limited that we do not even know what dangers we might be creating. Even as our technology begins to get out of control, we seek to develop it still further and look for technological solutions to problems that technology has created. And, somehow, as we thoughtlessly do all these things, we expect nature to remain unthreatening and to pose no serious threats to our continued survival.

We would do well to remember what the ancient peoples who made up the myths that we have been discussing knew so well—that Mother Earth is not always a benevolent goddess. On the contrary, she is quite capable of reacting to our insults by breeding monsters intent upon our destruction. Even when left alone she habitually unleashes awesome forces: as much energy is released in a thunderstorm or a small earthquake as there is in a hydrogen bomb explosion; the energy production in a hurricane is the approximate equivalent of one H-bomb per minute.

The cataclysms which take place upon the surface of the earth can be terrifying. However, they are as nothing compared to the events which take place on a cosmic scale. A *supernova explosion* in a nearby star, to mention just one possibility, could shower us with enough radiation to put an end to the entire human race, and to numerous other terrestrial species besides.

Nearby supernova explosions will inevitably take place. The next one might happen hundreds of millions of years in the future, or it might take place relatively soon. We don't know when it will occur, but we do know that it has happened in the past and that it will occur again in the future.

Astronomers believe that every star undergoes a phase of expansion and evolves into a *red giant* as it nears the end of its life. If our sun is a normal star, it will enter that stage about 5 billion years from now. It will expand until its surface lies at about the present orbit of Mars. Long before this happens the earth will be vaporized.

One would think that something that lies 5 billion years in the future is not an event that we should feel very concerned about. Recent research, however, has uncovered the possibility that the sun might not be a normal star. Scientists can no longer make predictions about its future behavior with as much confidence as they once thought they could. The sun, which was until recently thought to be so well understood, has turned out to be much more enigmatic than scientists had expected it to be. Astronomers used to believe that the sun was extremely stable, that it would continue to shine with constant brightness for a long time to come. Now no one can be sure that it might not suddenly become brighter, or dimmer, or fluctuate back and forth.

Events which take place within the earth can interact with those that unfold within the cosmic arena. For example, every now and then the earth's magnetic field decreases to a fraction of its normal value. When it does, we become especially vulnerable to the high-energy particles that are emitted by the sun. If there were any especially violent solar storms at a time when the magnetic field was low, the flux of solar particles falling on the earth could disrupt the ozone layer, causing the earth to be flooded with lethal ultraviolet radiation from the sun.

Similarly, although no one knows what the causes of ice ages are, it seems likely that astronomical events play some role. There is some evidence that ice ages can be correlated with variations and wobbles in the earth's orbit, and it has been suggested that interstellar dust might also be one of the culprits. The latter theory says that ice ages are more likely to happen when the motion of the sun about the center of the galaxy carries the solar system into one or another of the dust lanes associated with the spiral arms of the Milky Way. Since a number of terrestrial causes are also most likely involved, it seems safe to say that the production of ice ages is another area in which cosmic and terrestrial happenings interact and that technology will create hazards which will intensify the effects of these cosmic disasters. There is already evidence that a new ice age is beginning, and while it is not likely that it is being caused by air pollution, the massive quantities of chemicals that we pour into the atmosphere could conceivably create effects that will make the ice age more severe than it would otherwise be.

Aerosol sprays are beginning to have an effect upon the ozone layer. Within fifty years, those already in the atmosphere will destroy 15 per cent of the ozone. This will cause an increase of about 30 per cent in the intensity of ultraviolet radiation at the surface of the earth. Although this will increase the incidence of skin cancer and make sunburns more severe, it may not present any serious threat to the continued existence of the human race.

Suppose, however, that some natural event takes place which reduces the already weakened ozone layer still further. In such a case, our technology might turn out to have contributed to our destruction. A reduction in the magnetic field which normally would have no very significant effect could become a terrifying event if it acted upon natural defenses that were already weakened.

One should not, of course, discount the possibility that our technology alone will create some serious danger—a plague unleashed by an experiment with recombinant DNA (deoxyribonucleic acid) that got out of control, for example. It is much more likely, however, that the interaction of technology and natural events will bring about our destruction.

The technological age has existed for only a few hundred years; in a sense it is still in its infancy. Already it seems apparent that the more it "progresses," the more the dangers proliferate. We in the United States are already spending billions of dollars on attempts to control the pollution that we have produced. Eventually, a large part of our technological efforts and expenditures may be directed toward taming the very perils that we have created.

Thomas Hobbes's characterization of human life as something that is "solitary, poor, nasty, brutish, and short" is an apt description of what it would be like to live in a pre-technological society. Life without technology would not be pleasant or romantic. Anyone who thinks that it would should be reminded that, during the Stone Age, a person who reached forty was already old. Even in medieval times the average life expectancy came nowhere near the biblical three-score and ten; the majority of children did not even survive to adulthood. Those who did frequently fell victim to the plague, and even if one managed to survive to old age, life was not very comfortable, at least not by modern standards.

The solution to our problems lies not in dismantling our technology, but rather in curbing our obsessive compulsion to manipulate nature. This compulsion is thought by some to be very close to what Friedrich Nietzsche described as the "will to power." Whether the comparison is accurate or not, it certainly seems obvious that contemporary man generally views nature as something to be dominated rather than as an environment to be lived in.

Sooner or later the universe is going to destroy us. If we provoke it enough, the end may come within the next century or two. If we do not, we may survive for hundreds of millions of years. However, in one way or another, we will perish. Even if we someday go so far as to establish a galactic empire, we will still have to contend with the greatest natural disaster of all, the death of the universe.

Most likely, however, our particular species will disappear before the earth does and be replaced by another dominant species, which may or may not be intelligent. If anything, intelligence such as we possess might turn out to be a trait that

works against long-term survival. After we are gone, evolution may not care to repeat the experiment.

Whatever the beings are that replace us, they too will have to contend with the violent natural disasters that will inevitably take place. Time after time, the earth will be frozen by ice ages, suffer collisions with astronomical bodies, and be bombarded by radiation from supernovae. If the earth lasts long enough, it will collide with fragments of its own moon when the latter breaks up under the influence of tidal forces. And, finally, it will be vaporized when the sun evolves into a red giant.

2

THE EVOLUTION
AND DEATH OF THE SUN

Billions of years ago the universe contained nothing but hydrogen and helium gas dispersed more or less evenly through space. Then turbulent motions caused eddies to develop in the gas; some of these measured as much as thousands or millions of light-years in diameter. But for the action of gravitational forces, these tenuous clouds would have dissipated at once; in fact, it is fairly certain that this is just what happened to some of them. Others, however, grew more and more dense, ultimately condensing into galaxies and into clusters of galaxies.

There were not yet any stars. Gravity, however, continued to work. The clouds fragmented into smaller clumps. As these condensed also, gravitational forces became stronger, and the process of compression was accelerated. Finally, temperature and pressures in some of the now rather dense clouds became great enough for nuclear reactions to begin. One by one, stars began to light up the sky.

There were no observers to watch these dramatic events.

The heavy elements from which earthlike planets would later be formed did not yet exist. Carbon, nitrogen, oxygen, and the other important constituents of life had not yet been created. Nothing existed but interstellar gas, stars of various sizes, and gaseous clouds that were still compressing themselves through gravitational attraction. If there were any planets, they would have to have been gas giants like Jupiter and Saturn.

The smaller stars burned their nuclear fuel slowly. Some of them would have lifetimes of tens of billions of years and can still be seen by astronomers. The larger stars, on the other hand, had more voracious appetites. Some of them were up to 50,000 times as bright as the sun. The only way that they could achieve such a brightness was by burning up their fuel with a corresponding rapidity. Consuming themselves within a relatively short time, they exploded in the end and ejected into space the heavy elements that had been formed by the nuclear reactions in their cores. Among these elements were carbon, oxygen, nitrogen, silicon, and iron.

These substances mingled with the still plentiful hydrogen and helium as interstellar gas and dust. When second-generation stars began to form, these heavy elements were part of them. These elements also provided the raw materials from which planets with rocky crusts and metallic cores could be formed, planets on which life would have a chance to evolve.

The stars of the second and succeeding generations also came in all sizes. There were blue-white giants like Rigel which were destined to burn out in a few million years, countless billions of very small stars which would last almost as long as the universe itself, and vast numbers of medium-sized stars like the sun.

Scientists do not completely understand the process of star formation. Although they think that they know why the primordial hydrogen and helium gas condensed into galaxies, they do not yet have a good theoretical explanation of how the smaller clumps which were to become stars were created.

Astronomers have discovered regions, for example, in the Great Nebula in Orion, where the creation of stars is still taking place. Unfortunately, these regions are full of dust and gas which make observation difficult, and it is difficult to study the process in detail. Furthermore, stars that are bright enough for us to see are created in our galaxy only at about the rate of one every five hundred years. Astronomers consider themselves lucky to have observed one such star, FU Orionis, which "switched on" in 1936.

Obviously, the clouds of gas and dust that were to become *protostars* did separate out from the galactic cloud in some manner or another. If they hadn't, stars would not exist. Fortunately, the evolution of a star from this point onward is somewhat better understood. Although some details still need to be worked out, the current theory is probably correct in its broad outlines.

As gravity compressed the protostar that was to become the sun, pressure rose in its interior. At the same time, the release of gravitational energy caused the gas to heat up. The hot gas began to glow, radiating light and heat into space. Even though the temperature was not yet high enough for nuclear reactions to begin, the sun was, at this stage, emitting about 500 times as much energy as it is now. It shone with a luminosity that it will not again attain until it is near its death 5 billion years from now.

As the sun continued to contract, a process that took 20 or 30 million years, it gradually became less luminous. At the same time, temperatures in its core increased still further until a temperature of about 10 million degrees was reached.* At this point, nuclear fusion began, and the sun settled into its sedate middle age, a state that was to last for about 10 billion years. This is the orthodox theory; in Chap-

---

* Except when otherwise noted, temperatures are given in degrees Kelvin, or ° K. This is the same as the Celsius (° C) scale, except that temperatures are measured from absolute zero instead of from the freezing point of water. Absolute zero, or 0° K, is −273° C (−460° F. [Fahrenheit]).

ter 4 we will see that some astronomers are beginning to suspect that either there is something wrong with the standard
theory of stellar structure or that the sun may not be a normal star. However, enough stars have been observed to enable us to be fairly certain that the details of stellar evolution
which we are outlining cannot be too far wrong. We will
continue with the story, therefore, and put off a discussion of
the theoretical difficulties that have cropped up until later.

There are several kinds of nuclear burning which take
place in the sun. One of these, however, produces far more
energy than any of the others. This is the *proton-proton reaction*, a process consisting of three steps by which hydrogen
nuclei combine to form helium. A *proton* is nothing more
than the nucleus of a hydrogen atom, so "proton" and "hydrogen" are often used interchangeably in discussions of
processes which take place in stellar interiors.

In the first step of the proton-proton reaction, two hydrogen nuclei come together to form deuterium, or heavy hydrogen. The deuterium collides with another proton, forming
tritium, another form of heavy hydrogen.† Finally, two tritium nuclei fuse and form helium, releasing two protons as a
by-product of the reaction. The net result of this three-step
process is that four protons have combined to make helium.
The reaction is like the one which takes place in an H-bomb
explosion. The only difference is that bombs are made of
deuterium and tritium only; the first step, which is slow and
not very explosive, is bypassed.

When hydrogen is converted into helium, a small amount
of mass is lost; 4.0325 grams of hydrogen make only 4.0039
grams of helium. The remaining 0.0286 grams are converted
into energy, according to Albert Einstein's equation $E=mc^2$.

† Deuterium nuclei are made up of one proton and one neutron; tritium is
composed of one proton and two neutrons. Nuclei which have the same
number of protons but different numbers of neutrons are *isotopes* of the same
element.

Only a small quantity of matter is required to create enormous amounts of energy. For example, the sun has enough fuel to continue burning at its present rate for billions of years; at the end of its 10-billion-year life span less than one tenth of 1 per cent of its mass will have been lost. The sun does convert 4.5 million tons of mass into energy every second, but this amount is not very large compared to the sun's total mass of 2×10^{27} (the numeral 2 followed by twenty-seven zeros) tons.

Although stars like the sun seem to be very stable, they do undergo changes. If our ideas about stellar structure are correct, then the sun was about 40 per cent less luminous when the earth was formed 4.5 billion years ago than it is at present. During this time its brightness has gradually increased. It is also growing larger, but even more slowly; it is estimated that its radius has increased by about 4 per cent.

The sun will continue to grow larger and brighter in the future, but it will be some time before these changes have any significant effect on terrestrial life. About 1.5 billion years from now, however, the sun will begin to evolve more rapidly. At that time the supply of hydrogen fuel in the center of the sun will run out. There will still be sufficient hydrogen left elsewhere so that it can continue burning, but it will undergo changes which will cause its luminosity to increase at an ever more rapid rate.

When the central hydrogen is exhausted, a core of helium "ash" will form. Hydrogen fusion will then take place in a shell that surrounds this core. The core will contract, heating up in the process. The high temperatures will create increased pressures which will cause the sun to expand; paradoxically, it is the contraction of the core which causes an aging star to become larger.

The heating that is associated with the core contraction will cause hydrogen fusion in the surrounding shell to proceed faster, producing more heat and light. Five billion years from now the sun will have grown four times as bright as it is now, and its diameter will have increased by a factor of 3. It will be about to enter its red-giant stage.

The earth will not yet be vaporized, or engulfed by the growing sun, but it will cease to be habitable. By the time the sun reaches this stage, the temperatures on the surface of our planet will be so great that all the oceans will have boiled away.

It is not possible to estimate precisely when life will become impossible on earth. As the sun grows hotter, complex changes will take place in the atmosphere of the earth. It is likely that the so-called *greenhouse effect* caused by increased cloud cover will accelerate the heating process. Other changes might, however, have the opposite effect.

Although we cannot construct a time scale, it is possible to describe the changes that are likely to take place. At first they will be relatively modest. The increased solar radiation will evaporate a greater amount of water from the oceans, causing increased cloud cover. The polar ice caps will melt. Most likely, the various species living on the surface of the earth will undergo evolutionary changes, adapting themselves for life under the new conditions. Those which are unable to change rapidly enough will become extinct, and new species will replace them. It is unlikely that the human race will still exist at this time, but if it does, then we will almost certainly be dark-skinned; a large amount of skin pigmentation is likely to be necessary to provide protection against solar radiation.

As the sun grows hotter yet, conditions will change more rapidly. If any intelligent species live on the earth at this time, they may be able to engineer changes in the atmosphere which will cut off some of the solar energy and make the earth more livable. They will, however, only be delaying the destruction of the earth; it is not likely that changing the composition of the atmosphere can prevent it.

It is not possible to say very much about what these intelligent beings might be like, if indeed there are any. They may be our descendants, or *Homo sapiens* may have abandoned the earth by this time, giving other intelligent species the opportunity to evolve. We may have destroyed ourselves or have been eliminated by one or another of the cosmic cataclysms which will inevitably take place before this time. Finally, there is the possibility that the earth might be populated by a machine civilization. Artificial intelligence in computers may become a reality in the not too distant future. Within a few decades we should be able to endow computers with circuitry that equals the human brain in complexity. If machine intelligence is developed, it might survive catastrophes that would destroy us. Machines are less vulnerable to radiation and to climatic changes than any living organism.

Some of us tend to reject the idea of machine intelligence on emotional grounds, refusing to believe that any computer could ever be "conscious" or "intelligent." Such objections are, for the most part, untenable. While it may turn out that machine intelligence is impossible, until we manage to attain some understanding of what these things called "intelligence" and "consciousness" really are, we cannot rule out the possibility. Man has been struggling with the so-called mind-body problem for more than two thousand years; it is one of the most notorious problems in philosophy. Until we can come up with some reasonable solution to it, we should not make any pronouncements about the kinds of "bodies" in which "mind" can or cannot exist.

If any intelligent creatures exist on this planet when the sun becomes very hot a billion or several billion years in the future, they will probably differ from us in at least one important respect. Whatever they are, it is reasonable to assume that they will not share our irrationality and our capacity for self-destruction. A billion or more years of evolution should be sufficient to eliminate species with qualities like these. If evolution does not change us, we will inevitably be replaced by species better able to survive.

As the sun enters the red-giant stage, it will begin to evolve ever more rapidly. Its energy output will quickly become not four, but a thousand times as great as it is at present. The temperature on the earth will increase to approximately 1,200° (about 2,000° F), which is roughly the melting point of iron. For about 600 million years the sun will continue to expand, until its surface lies at about the present orbit of Mars. As it does, it will become even hotter and brighter. Only in the outer reaches of the solar system will life still be possible.

Astronomers believe that the sun will become a red giant because they are able to see the same process taking place in other stars. The preceding description of the future evolution of the sun is based less on chains of theoretical reasoning than it is on observations of other stars, which are presumed to be similar. There is no way of knowing, of course, that these stars have the same internal structure as our sun. However, until there is some evidence to the contrary, it is safe to assume that they do. The description of the sun as a red giant, in other words, depends upon the apparently reasonable assumption that stars tend to resemble one another. Since the time of Copernicus, astronomers have been reluctant to assume that there is anything very special about the earth or its sun.

It is not difficult to observe red giants in the sky. For one thing, they are intrinsically bright and therefore easy to see. For another, they exist in abundance. Star formation has been going on for 10 or 15 billion years or more, so it is possible to study stars at every point in their life cycles. As far as we can tell, the red-giant stage is a phase experienced by every star as it nears the end of its life.

The evolution of a star into a red giant is caused by an acceleration of the processes that have already been taking place. The hydrogen burning in the shell around the helium core proceeds at an ever more rapid rate. The output of heat increases, pressures rise still more, and the outer layers of the star are forced even further away from the core.

At present, the temperature at the core of the sun is about 15 million degrees. After 500 million years of red-giant growth, it will increase to 100 million degrees. When this point is reached, the helium in the sun's core will begin to undergo nuclear fusion. There will be sufficient heat energy to force helium nuclei together. In this *triple-helium* reaction, three helium nuclei will combine to form carbon. This will provide a fresh supply of energy, causing the sun to undergo changes even more violent than those which had been taking place before.

The onset of helium burning begins with a sudden burst of energy that astronomers call the *helium flash*. Then, as the sun adjusts to the effects of the helium explosion in its interior, it will undergo a partial collapse and briefly decrease its luminosity. The energy released by helium fusion will, however, quickly bring the collapse to a halt. The sun will again increase its size and light output. At the end of an additional 30 million years, it will have a diameter 400 times greater than that it possesses at present, and its light output will have increased by a factor of ten thousand.

When a red giant passes into the helium-burning stage, it consumes its fuel at a prodigious rate. The sun's helium will last for only 100 million years, an extremely short time compared to the 10 billion years that are required to exhaust the supply of hydrogen. When the helium is gone, the sun will gradually shrink and decrease in brightness until it becomes a tiny, dim *white dwarf*.

Astronomers have not yet been able to work out all the details of this process. They aren't sure how violent it will be or exactly how long it will take. They are certain, however, that it is inevitable. With no fuel left to burn, there will be no way that the sun will be able to maintain its bloated state.

As a star shrinks into a white dwarf, it may undergo explosions and may even throw off its outer layers, ejecting an envelope of hot gases called a *planetary nebula*. While it is known that many red giants eject stellar material at this stage, not all the details are well understood.

If a red giant is massive enough, it may undergo an especially spectacular explosion called a "supernova," but we can be reasonably certain that such a fate will not befall our sun. Supernovae take place only in stars that are much more massive than it is. Neither is the type of smaller outburst that is known as a *nova* likely to take place, if current theories are at all accurate. Novae are thought to be events which take place only in binary star systems.

As the sun transforms itself into a white dwarf, it will shrink to about 1 per cent of its present diameter, until it is about the size of the earth. As it does so, it will become so compressed that its density will be a million times as great as terrestrial rock. A chunk of solar material the size of a matchbox will weigh a ton, and a cupful will outweigh two dozen elephants.

At first a white dwarf is quite bright. The enormous temperatures generated during the red-giant stage cause it to glow with an initial luminosity fifty times as great as that of the present sun. However, it has, at this point, already begun to cool. Over a period of billions of years, white dwarfs grow progressively dimmer. Their color changes from white to dull red to black, as they evolve into *black dwarfs*, dark relics of dead suns.

The majority of the white dwarfs that astronomers observe are quite dim, no more than a few per cent of the sun's brightness. It would not be unreasonable to compare them to the embers that may persist for many hours after a fire has ceased to produce any visible flame.

An advanced technological civilization would be able to make use of the heat and light emitted by a white dwarf for quite some time. It would only be necessary to move in close enough to feel its warmth, exactly analogous to the way in which we move closer to a dying fire.

It is survival during the red-giant stage that would be difficult. However, the difficulties could presumably be overcome. Although the earth will not be very hospitable to life, the moons of Jupiter might be quite habitable. Space colonies might provide another solution. It is even conceivable that our successors might decide to move the earth itself. There is no reason why an entire planet could not be nudged into progressively wider orbits as the sun grew hotter. If the process were stretched out over a period of 100 million years, it would only be necessary to increase the speed of the earth by about a hundredth of a centimeter per second every year. To be sure, this would require the expenditure of enormous quantities of energy, the equivalent of that which would be produced by the explosion of billions of hydrogen bombs.

A civilization existing 5 billion years in the future might consider such a task to be entirely feasible, yet they might prefer not to carry it out. Perhaps moving the earth is the kind of violent solution that only humans would think of. Although our hypothetical future race might have the technological capability for something like this, it might have an outlook on nature that is different than our own; it might have enough humility to abhor such extreme solutions.

If the earth were moved, this would provide only a temporary solution. Its inhabitants would hardly have adjusted its position to the energy output of the red-giant sun when they would have to think of moving it again in anticipation of the helium flash. This time, the earth would have to be moved more quickly, for the sun will begin to change much more rapidly once it reaches the helium-burning stage.

There would be other problems also. For example, if the sun ejected a planetary nebula, the earth's atmosphere might be blown away. Other violent events taking place on the sun's surface might cause the earth to be bathed in dangerous radiation. And then, when the sun began to shrink into a dwarf, it would be necessary to reverse the process and bring the earth closer to the sun.

It would be possible, of course, to move the earth out of the solar system entirely and to go looking for another suitable sun. A far simpler solution, however, would be to leave the earth entirely. Artificial space colonies, which have already been mentioned, would be one solution. Another would be to live on other astronomical bodies.

The American physicist Freeman Dyson thinks that we will eventually colonize the comets, and perhaps even grow trees on them. Since the gravity on comets is low, there are few limits on the height to which vegetation could grow. Dyson envisions cometary trees that rise hundreds of miles into space, giving each of these small bodies an appearance not unlike that of a sprouting potato.

The idea is not so outlandish as it sounds. A "halo" of something like 100 billion comets surrounds the solar system. Although some comets have elongated orbits that take them nearly halfway to the nearest star, only a few ever approach the sun near enough to become luminescent. This is the reason why, although comets are by far the most numerous objects in the universe, only a small number ever become visible to the casual observer on earth.

Comets are made up of ice, frozen ammonia, and dust particles. The ice could be melted to support life. As long as a comet did not approach too near the sun, its constituents would remain frozen together. Thus its inhabitants would live either on or beneath the solid surface. According to Dyson, plants might be genetically altered to enable them to be grown in space. They might be modified in such a way that they would spread enormous leaves over wide areas to catch the sun's dim illumination.

While it is fairly certain that the sun will eventually evolve into a red giant (there seems to be no other fate that could befall it), we cannot guess what the inhabitants of the earth will do about this. It is possible to imagine what we *might* do, but we will not be here. The probability that after 5 billion years of evolution any beings resembling humans still exist, can be said to be vanishingly small. When the sun dies, "we" will not be around to see it.

3

SUPERNOVAE

Man often likes to think that he has mastered the forces of nature. It is doubtful, however, that we could be so smug if we had, during civilized times, experienced any of the astronomical catastrophes which regularly take place in the universe. When nature becomes aroused, it can be awesome, and we should count ourselves lucky that we do not yet know how terrifying it can be.

When we imagine worldwide disaster, we ordinarily think in terms of some such event as a nuclear holocaust. We do so with good reason; the present stockpiles of nuclear weapons have a destructive power which is the equivalent of 10 tons of TNT for every person on this planet. The fear that some of these weapons will soon begin to go off, especially if nuclear proliferation continues, is not an unreasonable one.

Yet, however destructive a nuclear holocaust might be, its long term effects would be mild compared to those of a nearby supernova explosion. If a star thirty light-years—about 200 trillion miles—away were to become a supernova, the en-

ergy falling on the surface of the earth might be the equivalent of that produced by a hundred thousand or even 1 million H-bombs. The entire human race might very well be
obliterated.

We would experience no "blast" effects; the shock waves
which manage to propagate through interstellar gas are tenuous things and would not be able to generate any measurable
pressure waves in the air. A supernova would not flatten any
buildings. Neither would it cause any fires; the heat that it
produced would be spread out over too long a time period
even to bring about a noticeable rise in the earth's surface
temperature.

The radioactive fallout, however, would be intense. Cosmic rays would continue to bombard the earth for hundreds
or thousands of years. In order to survive, human beings
might have to live underground, or establish colonies at the
bottom of the oceans. If we did not have time to make the
necessary preparations, we might, like the dinosaurs, become
extinct. A nearby supernova explosion is one of the possible
explanations for the end of the age of reptiles.

Supernovae are rare events; it is estimated that one takes
place in our galaxy only about once every fifty or one hundred years. Since there are more than 100 billion stars in
our Milky Way galaxy and since only a few hundred of these
lie within a thirty-light-year radius of the earth, it is obvious
that nearby supernova explosions don't take place very often.
Indeed, it has been estimated that they might happen only
once every billion years or so; there could have been as few as
three or four during the entire 4.5 billion year history of our
planet.

Rare events do, however, happen sooner or later. Every star
larger than a certain minimum mass is a potential bomb. Although some of these, for unknown reasons, escape a violent
fate, most do end their lives in supernova explosions. As they
are blown apart, for a short time they radiate more energy

than an entire galaxy. We can expect that the earth will have to endure the effects of this energy several times between the present and the time that the sun dies.

A nearby supernova explosion does not, of course, have to lie at a distance of exactly thirty light-years. We can expect that there will be explosions at distances of twenty-five, forty, sixty, or two hundred light-years, and at virtually every other distance as well. Those that are farther away will produce effects that are less intense, but they will happen more often. A supernova at a distance of sixty light-years, for example, would probably not destroy us, but it might make life uncomfortable for at least a century or two. We can reasonably expect to experience something like this ten or twenty times between now and the time that the sun becomes a red giant.

The terms "nova" and "supernova" take their names from a book by the sixteenth-century Danish astronomer Tycho Brahe, a forerunner of Galileo and Keppler who contributed mightily to the success of the Copernican revolution. Tycho's book *De Nova Stella* ("On the New Star") described a supernova which became visible in 1572 and which could be seen in the sky for several years thereafter.

The name was, perhaps, an unfortunate one. Novae and supernovae are not "new" stars at all; they are stars which suddenly flare up after they have been in existence for millions or billions of years. Moreover, the terms "nova" and "supernova" describe two entirely different kinds of event. A nova is, by astronomical standards, not an especially violent happening. And while a supernova blows a star apart, a nova is usually a recurrent process that can happen hundreds or thousands of times in the same place.

Ordinary novae are quite common and not especially bright. While a nearby supernova would give considerably more light than a full moon, novae rarely become as brilliant as the brightest star in the sky; the more distant ones are not even visible to the naked eye. Novae are detected in our galaxy about forty times a year, which makes them thousands of times more common than supernovae.

It is believed that novae are flare-ups that take place in binary systems in which one of the two stars is a small, hot, white dwarf. If the dwarf's companion is a very massive star and if the two are close enough to one another, then gravitational forces will cause the dwarf to pull hot gas from the surface of its companion. When this gas falls on the white dwarf, the outburst occurs.

It is possible that nova-like outbursts might sometimes take place in stars, like the sun, that are not members of binary systems. However, it is not likely that a nova will ever have the slightest effect on life inhabiting this planet. If the sun ever exhibits an outburst of this character, it is likely to happen only after the red-giant stage has been reached. Since by that time the earth will have already been sterilized—or vaporized—a nova would not be an especially catastrophic event, at least not from our somewhat parochial point of view. Since novae do not produce enough energy to create any significant effects across interstellar distances, we wouldn't have to worry if such explosions took place even in the nearest stars. The science fiction stories once written about nova explosions which threatened some planetary civilization or another would not be credible today, at least not to anyone familiar with contemporary astronomy.

During the last two thousand years, there have been a number of galactic supernovae which have been visible from the earth. In A.D. 185, for example, astronomers of the Chinese Han dynasty observed a supernova and carefully recorded the event in court chronicles. It appeared to have a brightness of about "half a mat," they noted, and it was "of five colors." Astronomers would like to know more about this event, but unfortunately no one seems to know how bright a "mat" was, and so it is difficult to make use of this ancient piece of information.

In A.D. 1054 an especially spectacular supernova was seen in China. Shortly after its appearance, the chief astronomer of the Sung dynasty made the following report to his emperor: "Prostrating myself, I have observed the appearance of a guest star; on the star there was slightly iridescent yellow color. Respectfully, according to the dispositions for emperors, I have prognosticated, and the result said: The guest star does not infringe upon Aldebaran; this shows that a Plentiful One is Lord, and that the country has a Great Worth. I request that this be given to the Bureau of Historiography to be preserved."

Although this supernova ceased to be visible nearly a thousand years ago, its spectacular remnants can still be seen today. Hot gases from the A.D. 1054 explosion are still hurtling outward into space. Light from nearby stars make them visible as a nebulosity in the constellation Taurus known as the *Crab Nebula.* In its center, where there was once a massive star, there is now only a small, dark radio-emitting object known to astronomers as NP 0532.

This supernova did not, of course, explode in 1054; that is the date on which its light reached the earth. The Crab Nebula is six thousand light-years away, hence the explosion took place around 5000 B.C. It became visible only after the light had spent six thousand years traveling toward us through space.

Although the Chinese carefully recorded every unusual astronomical event, noting novae and comets as well as supernovae, far less attention was paid to such things in the West. The only two supernovae which have been carefully studied by European astronomers are those which were seen in A.D. 1572 and 1604. Since that time, there have been no supernovae in the Milky Way galaxy that were visible from the earth. If any supernova explosions took place in our galaxy at all, they happened in regions where their light was obscured by interstellar dust.

The telescope was not invented until 1608, four years after the last Milky Way supernova was seen, hence astronomers have never had the opportunity to take a close look at one of these rare explosions. While they are able to detect ten to twenty supernova outbursts per year in other galaxies, these are quite far away. For example, the Great Galaxy in Andromeda, the nearest of all the large galaxies, lies at a distance of nearly 2 million light-years. Even the largest telescopes can resolve few stars at such distances. Astronomers have been able to see the stars which become supernovae only after they have exploded. No one has ever had the chance to look at a star that was destined to become a supernova before it blew up. Astronomers have been waiting for a supernova in an already catalogued star for some time now; they fear that they may have to wait hundreds of years more.

As a result, no one is absolutely certain as to what kinds of stars become supernovae. Until that already known star is observed to explode, there will be no observational data. At present, therefore, it is necessary to depend on theoretical models and on computer computations if one wants to know what is happening when supernova explosions take place.

Naturally there is a certain amount of scientific controversy about the results. In order to do calculations in theoretical physics, it is always necessary to make certain simplifying assumptions; otherwise the mathematics becomes too difficult. Sometimes no one really knows which assumptions are correct, and thus it is possible for different theorists to arrive at different answers.

Fortunately, in the case of supernovae there are some things which can be assumed with a reasonable degree of certainty. It is known that supernovae are the death throes of massive stars. A supernova shines, for a short time, with the brightness of an entire galaxy; a small- or medium-sized star could not produce that much light. Also, since supernova remnants have been observed, the amount of stellar material thrown off in the explosion can be calculated; it turns out that this can be as much as ten or a hundred solar masses.

No one knows exactly how big a star has to be in order to explode as a supernova. Theoretical calculations indicate that the stellar core must be at least 1.4 solar masses, but the core is only the inner part of a star. Also, stars explode as supernovae only after they have gone through the red-giant stage, and astronomers are not sure how much mass a star can lose while it is a red giant.

It is sometimes assumed that stars which have more than three or four times the mass of our sun are potential supernovae. Although this is admittedly only a guess, the true figure can't be very much higher or lower. "Three or four solar masses" is, in all probability, a reasonably good "ballpark" approximation.

In order to describe a supernova explosion in detail, it will be necessary to backtrack a little and discuss in more detail some of the processes that take place in a star while it is a red giant. We learned in the last chapter that a red giant was a star which was rapidly exhausting its hydrogen fuel and forming a helium core. Depending upon the size of the star, there are several things which can happen next.

In small stars, no very spectacular events take place. The hydrogen eventually gives out, and the red giant gradually shrinks into a white dwarf as its nuclear fires die. Most of the stars that are smaller than the sun end their lives in this way; there is no helium flash because temperatures never become high enough to ignite the helium core.

In stars about the size of the sun, the process is, as we have seen, a more complicated one. When the temperature reaches 100 million degrees, the helium begins to undergo fusion. For a short time, the luminosity of the star increases dramatically and its color changes from red to blue. But the helium is consumed at so prodigious a rate that the supply is soon exhausted. Such a star also settles down and shrinks into a white dwarf. Its fate is the same as that of a star which never became hot enough to ignite the helium to begin with.

The more massive stars, those with supernova potential, refuse to die such relatively quiet deaths when their helium runs out. Instead, the forces of gravity go to work once again, contracting the core once more and pushing the central temperatures still higher. If the star is large enough, the temperature in the core will rise to around a billion degrees, and heavier elements such as carbon and oxygen will begin to undergo fusion.

More and more elements are built up until most of the material in the core has been converted into iron, the most stable element of all. There is no way that nuclear reactions can proceed any further, for energy is absorbed, not released, when heavier nuclei are formed. To be sure, conditions are so chaotic that heavier elements are produced in small amounts, but they tend to be blasted apart almost as soon as they are created. In order to form an iron core, the star has used one nuclear fuel after another. Once the iron stage is reached, there is no way that fusion can continue.

In order to learn something about the conditions that exist in a star at this stage, it is necessary to depend on computer calculations. Even if we were able to observe a supernova in our own galaxy, there would be no way to see into the star's interior. There is, therefore, no way that we can determine exactly how high the temperatures and pressures there are now. We only know that they must be truly awesome. According to one estimate, the temperature of the iron core is a thousand times greater than that which exists at the center of an H-bomb explosion, and the pressure is a trillion times greater than at the bottom of the earth's deepest oceans.

Yet the temperature and pressure of the star are to rise still more. When all the fuel is gone, the core contracts once again under the action of gravitational forces. The pressure continues to go up and the temperature rises to an almost unimaginable 8 billion degrees. *Gamma rays* are produced in this thermal holocaust, and the iron begins to break up under their bombardment. Within the space of a few minutes, nearly all the iron which had been laboriously built up in complicated processes lasting millions of years disintegrates into helium.

When the iron breaks apart, it suddenly takes back all the energy that was released during its formation. The disappearance of such vast quantities of energy causes a sudden cooling of the core. The enormous pressures vanish, and the entire stellar core collapses in the space of a few seconds. This causes the outer layers of the star to fall inward in a vast implosion. Then, almost at once, they rebound, blowing the star apart.

The explosion takes place so quickly that the dying star increases in luminosity until it is billions of times as bright as the sun. Theory is unable to describe all the complicated processes that are now taking place. Observations of supernovae in other galaxies do, however, tell us that the energy output in a supernova explosion is unequalled by anything in the universe. First, there is an intense burst of X-*rays*, lasting perhaps one hour. As the X-rays fade, visible light and ultraviolet radiation increase in intensity, reaching a peak in perhaps twenty days. At the same time, stellar material is hurled into space at velocities of 6,000 to 18,000 miles per second.

If the nearest star became a supernova, it would appear to be nearly as bright as the sun. Although a supernova thirty light-years away would be somewhat dimmer, it would still be a thousand times as bright as the full moon. After about a month, such a supernova would begin to dim, but even so it would remain a prominent feature of the night sky for years.

If all the light produced in a supernova explosion were emitted at once, there would be a flash of such intensity that no life on earth could survive it. Even after traveling 200 trillion miles through space, it could easily incinerate every combustible material on the face of the earth and consume every bit of oxygen in the atmosphere.

Fortunately, the light would not be given off all at once. Spread out over a period of months or years, it would have little effect, except perhaps to make street lights unnecessary at night. The ultraviolet radiation that accompanies the visible light would not be dangerous either; most of it would be absorbed by the ozone layer of the atmosphere. The real menace, cosmic radiation, would not arrive until years or decades after the light of the supernova had faded from the sky. This radiation would not fall upon us at once, but when it did, our continued survival would become problematical.

The term *cosmic ray* was coined early in the twentieth century, when scientists discovered that the earth was being constantly bombarded by a mysterious radiation that was coming from all directions of space. Since, at the time, no one understood exactly what this radiation was, it was called "cosmic," after its apparent source.

As knowledge of nuclear physics increased, it became possible to determine exactly what cosmic rays were. They turned out to be energetic particles, mostly protons and electrons, which struck the earth's atmosphere at velocities approaching the speed of light. As they did, they produced showers of secondary particles which cascaded down to the earth's surface.

If anything, these findings only made them seem more mysterious, for it wasn't clear how they could have been accelerated to such high velocities. Years passed and theories were developed which showed that the cosmic-ray particles could have been accelerated in the magnetic fields that stretch between the stars in interstellar space. Their origin, however, remained a mystery.

Finally, in the 1960s, scientists began to realize that cosmic rays could be created in supernova explosions. Calculations showed that the magnetic fields produced by a dying star could accelerate the particles to high velocities. It was hypothesized that supernovae were the source of most, if not all, cosmic rays that fell on the earth. The fact that they seemed to come from all directions created no theoretical difficulties. On the contrary, this fact was easy to explain. The universe has existed for 10 or 20 billion years, enough time for billions of supernovae to explode in all parts of space. Cosmic rays come from all directions because there have been supernovae everywhere. Those rays that fail to strike a star or a planet simply go on traveling through space for billions and billions of years. Under such circumstances, it would be surprising if the cosmic-ray background did not average itself out and seem to be of almost unvarying intensity.

Cosmic rays constitute a significant part of the radiation background that is present everywhere on the earth. It is this background which produces genetic mutations in every living organism and which makes evolution possible. To be sure, part of this background comes from the natural radioactivity of elements in the crust of the earth. It is clear, however, that without cosmic rays, evolution would have progressed at a much slower pace. In the absence of cosmic rays, it is not likely that the earth would have yet evolved any creature as complex or as intelligent as man.

However, cosmic radiation also produces effects that are anything but beneficial. The vast majority of the mutations which it induces are harmful. A few do create new evolutionary material, but these mutations are rare compared to those which can cause a major or a minor disability, or make an early death likely. Natural selection has always been faced with the difficult task of weeding out the harmful mutations before it could produce evolutionary change by operating on the "good" ones.

If the mutation rate was to rise to high enough a level, selection would hardly have a chance to operate at all. The "bad" mutations would proliferate, killing an increasingly large number of individuals and making it difficult for a species to reproduce in sufficient numbers to maintain a constant population. Something like this may have happened to the dinosaurs. It is not likely that any event took place which killed them all at once. If they simply reproduced in smaller numbers every year, this would have been sufficient to cause their extinction.

A threefold-to-tenfold increase in radiation is sufficient to double the mutation rate in most large species. Since cosmic rays from a supernova might cause the radiation levels on the surface of the earth to increase by as much as a factor of 100, it is obvious that the results would be catastrophic if the bombardment continued for any significant period of time. It is quite possible that neither man nor any of the other large land mammals would survive.

Although the cosmic rays would not reach us as quickly as a supernova's light, they would linger for a much longer period of time. Their time of arrival would be delayed by the fact that cosmic rays do not travel in a straight line; instead they bounce around in the magnetic fields that permeate space. This very effect, however, would ensure that they remained at peak intensity for as long as a century. Even then they would not fade away completely; cosmic radiation could remain at levels that were higher than normal for millennia.

If human beings somehow managed to live through such intense fallout and produce viable offspring, their problems would only be beginning. There would be mutations in all terrestrial species, including plants and microorganisms. Mutated viruses might create plagues against which we would have no resistance, and many of our food crops might become mutated to such a degree that they would become inedible or impossible to cultivate.

There would be other, equally serious, problems. During the past few years, some scientists have speculated that cosmic radiation from a supernova could cause certain nitrogen oxides to form in the atmosphere and that these oxides could deplete the ozone layer. Since it is the ozone which shields us from the sun's ultraviolet rays, the effects could be disastrous. If the ozone layer was to disappear completely, ultraviolet radiation could sterilize the entire surface of our planet, killing all life except that living in the depths of the ocean. If any such event took place, we might have to build underground cities or set up colonies at the bottom of the sea to have any chance to survive. In such a case, we might return to the surface of the earth centuries later, only to find that the land areas of our planet had been transformed into enormous deserts.

If a nearby supernova took place in the immediate future, there might be no human survivors at all. Life would, however, continue in the oceans, since water is an effective shield against radioactivity. So perhaps the human race will eventually go the way of the dinosaurs, leaving the earth to the whales and the dolphins. Or perhaps it is the cockroach that will survive us. The cockroach reached its present evolutionary form 250 million years ago, which makes it one of the most successful life forms on the surface of the earth. Roaches have almost certainly survived catastrophes of various kinds which would be sufficient to destroy humanity. The cockroach might die in the supernova fallout, too, but its past success certainly indicates that it would have a better chance of survival than we would.

4

THE
SOLAR NEUTRINO
PROBLEM

According to current theories of stellar evolution, we can expect that the sun will remain reasonably stable until it becomes a red giant 5 billion years from now. It may gradually grow hotter over a period of billions of years, but there will be no sudden changes in its luminosity. Thus, *if these theories are correct*, there will be no danger of any violent changes in the sun's behavior that might endanger life on earth.

The italicized words are important, for in recent years scientists have uncovered a large, unexplained disagreement between supposedly well-established theory and experiment. Some astronomers are beginning to believe that there may be something very wrong with our theories of stellar structure. Others have suggested that the sun may not be a normal star.

To date, no satisfactory explanation of the discrepancy has been found. While a little more than a decade ago the theory of stellar evolution was considered a dry subject, today it is a field of considerable controversy. Once it was believed that all the important questions in this area had been answered;

today the crisis has grown to such proportions that some scientists have begun to question basic principles that had been previously thought to be established beyond any possible doubt.

It is impossible to say what implications all of this might have for our ideas about the future evolution of the sun. Until the theoretical crisis is resolved, we cannot be certain that the sun might not be growing colder, or hotter, or engaging in unpredictable fluctuations. It may continue to be stable for another 5 billion years, as conventional theory predicts, or it may suddenly change. If it does change, we have no way of saying how serious the effects might be.

It should be emphasized that there is, at present, no observational evidence of any variation in the brightness of the sun. However, many astronomers feel that they can no longer have much confidence in the prospect of long-term solar stability. And small changes could have very significant effects; it has been estimated, for example, that a decrease in solar luminosity of only a few per cent would be sufficient to trigger another ice age.

The trouble began in the late 1960s when Raymond Davis, Jr., an American astrophysicist from the Brookhaven National Laboratory, set up experimental apparatus designed to measure certain subnuclear particles called *neutrinos* produced by nuclear reactions in the sun. Davis found that there were many fewer neutrinos than theory predicted. At first it had appeared that there might be none at all; the experimental uncertainties were such that it was only possible to place upper limits on the number of particles detected. Then, as the experiment was refined, it became apparent that the neutrinos were there, but in much smaller numbers than theory predicted.

Initially, many astronomers ignored Davis' results, hoping that it would be discovered that there was something wrong with the experiment. But the problem did not go away. The neutrino-detection experiment has been tested and improved, and the accuracy of the measurements has been increased. There is no escaping the conclusion that, somewhere along the line, erroneous assumptions have been incorporated into theories of solar structure. Until scientists find out what these incorrect assumptions are, we will not have any satisfactory theoretical description of the sun's structure and behavior.

The neutrino is one of the stranger particles discovered by modern physics. Possessing neither electric charge nor mass but traveling at the speed of light, it is one of the most elusive particles known. So great is its penetrating power that a neutrino could pass through a block of lead stretching from the earth to the nearest star without interacting with a single atom. The neutrino is so difficult to detect that, although its existence was first postulated in 1931 by the Austrian-born physicist Wolfgang Pauli, it wasn't observed experimentally until 1956. To get an idea as to how rarely neutrinos interact with matter, consider the following: As you read this book, trillions of neutrinos pass through your body every second; yet only a handful, probably no more than five or six, will interact with any of your constituent atoms during your lifetime.

One might think that if neutrinos are that hard to observe, it would not be possible to have much confidence in experiments designed to detect them. This is not true; neutrinos have been seen in the laboratory. It is only necessary to create a very intense neutrino beam with a particle accelerator and to wait until one interacts with an atom in the target upon which the beam has been directed. It may be necessary to wait some time, but the collisions can be observed.

When Davis set out to make an attempt to detect neutrinos coming from the sun, he found that he had set himself a Herculean task. In the first place, the experiment could not be carried out on the surface of the earth. If it were, the experimental apparatus would be contaminated by cosmic rays which would produce nuclear reactions that would mask any effects the neutrinos might have. The only way that an experiment could be performed would be to set up the equipment deep underground. Next, although it seemed that there was a good chance of capturing neutrinos by allowing them to interact with chlorine, it was obvious that hundreds of tons of the gas would be required.

Fortunately it was not necessary to use chlorine gas. Calculations showed that a detection tank containing 100,000 gallons of a chlorine-containing liquid such as perchloroethylene —ordinary cleaning fluid—would give the experiment a reasonable chance of success. And the background of cosmic rays could be screened out if the tank were set up at the bottom of a deep mine shaft. Unlike cosmic rays, neutrinos would pass through the earth unhindered until they were caught in the cleaning fluid. Even if there was only one neutrino interaction per day, it appeared that methods could be developed by which neutrino capture could be detected.

Together with the American physicist John Bahcall of the California Institute of Technology, who had originally suggested the experiment in 1964, Davis assembled a team of scientists. A cylindrical tank twenty feet in diameter and forty-eight feet long was constructed 4,850 feet underground in the Homestake Gold Mine in Lead, South Dakota. Other scientific equipment was set up, and in 1968 the experiment was begun.

To the lay person it might seem astonishing that scientists would want to go to so much trouble just to catch a few neutrinos, but there were reasons why the experiment was extremely important. Until it was made, there existed no way of looking into the center of the sun to see whether the nuclear reactions which theory said should be taking place were actually present. When the neutrino experiment was initially performed, no one had any serious doubts about existing theoretical models. Astronomers were sure that the neutrino count would turn out to be just what had been predicted. Scientists consider it important, however, to check theoretical predictions whenever possible. Without constant interaction between theory and experiment, there could be no such thing as science as we know it.

Prior to 1968, all our knowledge of the sun came from observations of its surface. These observations told astronomers how bright the sun was and enabled them to determine its size. Spectroscopic analysis gave information on the chemical composition of its surface layers. They could tell nothing, however, about the core where the nuclear reactions took place which were supposedly producing the sun's light and heat. The sun is so large and so dense that it takes approximately 2 million years for light that is produced in the core to make its way to the surface. Light rays bounce back and forth in the solar material; they are absorbed and reemitted over and over again by atoms in the various layers of the sun. Thus the energy that the sun produces is able to emerge only after it has traveled a long and tortuous path.

Neutrinos, on the other hand, make their way from the core to the surface without hindrance. The detector set up by Davis and his co-workers was in effect a "neutrino telescope" that allowed scientists to see into the sun for the very first time. There was no danger, incidentally, that the neutrinos detected would be coming, not from the sun, but from elsewhere in the universe. It was obvious that the difference in intensity between a beam of solar neutrinos and any others that might happen along would be roughly equivalent to the difference between sunlight and starlight. If any nonsolar neutrinos interacted with the cleaning fluid that was used as detection material, this event would happen so rarely that it could not possibly affect the results in any significant way.

The chemical formula for cleaning fluid is C_2Cl_4—each molecule containing two carbon and four chlorine atoms. About 75 per cent of the chlorine that exists in nature occurs as an isotope called chlorine 35; most of the remaining 25 per cent is chlorine 37. The two isotopes are chemically identical. The only difference between them is that one is a little heavier than the other; a chlorine 37 nucleus contains two extra neutrons. There is nothing mysterious about this. Most elements have a number of different isotopes. The uranium that is mined from the earth, for example, is about 99 per cent U-238 and one per cent U-235; the oxygen in the air is made up of oxygen 16 and oxygen 18.

Although different isotopes will exhibit the same chemical behavior, they will ordinarily undergo nuclear reactions in different ways. U-235 is fissionable, while U-238 is not. If one wishes to use it to make bombs, the latter must first be converted to plutonium in nuclear reactors. And only chlorine 37 can be used to detect neutrinos.

Chlorine 37 atoms do not capture neutrinos very frequently. However, if one has enough chlorine, these interactions are detectable. When a neutrino collides with chlorine 37, it transforms the latter into argon 37, a radioactive gas. If this gas is collected, the number of argon 37 atoms that are present can be measured simply by using devices designed to detect the presence of radioactivity.

If all this were as simple as it sounds, the experiment would have been performed long before 1968. Now, it is not difficult to collect argon 37 or to measure the number of argon atoms present. When argon 37 undergoes radioactive decay, it emits an electron and individual electrons can be detected quite easily. The reason the experiment is difficult to perform is that neutrinos interact with chlorine so rarely that enormous quantities of the material are required. Even though Davis' 100,000-gallon tank contained about 10^{31} (1 followed by thirty-one zeros) chlorine atoms, only a few neutrino interactions were expected to take place per day. If the tank had been appreciably smaller, it might have been necessary to wait months or even years before the first capture took place.

The number of neutrinos captured can be expressed in *solar neutrino units*, or SNU. One SNU (pronounced "snew") is defined to be one capture per second for every 10^{36} target atoms; this corresponds, in Davis' experiment, to the creation of 1 atom of argon 37 every five days. When the solar neutrino experiment was begun, the theorists who made calculations about processes in the sun expected a counting rate as high as 30 SNU. There was astonishment in the scientific community, therefore, when Davis reported that the actual capture rate was no more than 3 SNU, and probably less.

Although some astronomers hoped that there would turn out to be a hidden defect in the experiment, this possibility seemed less and less likely as time went on. Like any good experimental scientist, Davis had thoroughly tested his equipment. He also repeated the experiment numerous times in order to improve the accuracy of the results. He checked his results by deliberately introducing argon into his tank. When he collected it by flushing the apparatus with helium gas, he found that the argon could be detected with about 90 per cent efficiency. If the neutrinos had been producing as much argon 37 as theory said they would, he certainly would have seen it.

The theorists made a considerable effort to bring theory and experiment into agreement. They refined the accuracy of their calculations. Discovering that small changes in conditions encountered in the center of the sun could produce large variations in the number of neutrinos created, they lowered their estimates of the neutrino production rate. They came up with a new figure: 6 SNU. Certain theoretical uncertainties indicated that this figure might be in error by plus or minus 2 SNU. The new theoretical prediction, therefore, was 4–8 SNU. The discrepancy between this and the experimental value of 3 was not so bad after all. It was hoped that further improvements in both theory and experiment would remove it.

This is not what happened. After ten years of experimentation, Davis came up with an experimental result that was more accurate than any which he had obtained before. The observed neutrino capture rate was 1.75 SNU. There was some experimental uncertainty, but the true value had to be somewhere between 1.35 and 2.15. Meanwhile, the best theoretical calculations were found to predict a result of about 5 SNU. There was no longer any way to explain away the fact that theory and experiment were not in agreement. Astronomers and physicists alike began to realize that they were confronted with a scientific crisis of major proportions.

When the discrepancy first became apparent, everyone seemed to want to put the blame on someone else. The astronomers suggested that perhaps the physicists didn't understand fundamental processes as well as they thought they did. The physicists replied that the physics involved was elementary. It must be the astronomers, they said, who had a theory that didn't work. It was becoming obvious that someone's theory was in danger of crumbling. It was only natural that physicists and astronomers alike found themselves hoping that it would be the other guy's.

Once scientists got over their initial dismay, they set to work to find explanations for the missing neutrinos. So far, no one has come up with any that seem to work. The puzzle remains a puzzle, although virtually every possible explanation has been tried. It has been suggested that something might be happening to the neutrinos on their way from the sun to the earth, that nuclear reactions in the sun have slowed down or ceased, and even that the sun may contain a *black hole*.* But there is, as yet, no explanation that seems to work.

Many of the ideas that have been put forward have been

---

* A black hole is a massive object with a gravitational field so intense that nothing, not even light, can escape from its surface. Black holes will be discussed in greater detail in Chapter 9.

suggestions concerning possible modifications of ideas about solar structure. Rapid internal rotation in the sun could reduce the neutrino flux, as could intense magnetic fields or a pure helium core. The theoretical models developed from such assumptions, however, have not proved to be satisfactory; either they are not consistent with other experimental observations, are not stable for long periods, or violate generally accepted concepts. It has also been suggested that the sun periodically undergoes a kind of mixing which causes the core to cool and nuclear reactions to stop. However, no one has been able to suggest any satisfactory mechanism by which such a process might take place.

At present, one of the most reasonable-sounding suggestions is that the interior of the sun is devoid of heavy elements. If this was the case, radiation would escape from the sun's core more readily. This would, in turn, reduce the central temperature and slow down the reactions producing the largest number of neutrinos. Heavy elements are, however, observed on the sun's surface. If this model is to be made convincing, someone must explain why they exist there and not in the core. Some attempts have been made, but none is generally accepted.

Every now and then, science encounters some phenomenon for which it can find no reasonable explanation. When this happens, a state of scientific crisis is created, which persists until someone comes up with an apparently "unreasonable" solution that turns out to be true. Science, as Thomas Kuhn has pointed out in *The Structure of Scientific Revolutions*, does not develop by a simple process of accretion. It may be possible to make progress for a considerable period of time by accumulating data and working out the details of accepted theory, but there must inevitably come a point where data is gathered which cannot be reconciled to existing theory. The old paradigms begin to break down and a crisis is precipitated. All is chaos until some revolutionary new theory is proposed and accepted.

It is not yet clear that the solar neutrino problem has caused any such scientific revolution. It may be that someone will yet work out a solution to the problem which requires that only minor modifications be made in our ideas about solar structure. On the other hand, Davis' attempts to detect solar neutrinos may have pushed us in such a direction that we are on the brink of some revolutionary discovery. It would not be inappropriate, therefore, to examine two of the more "outlandish" theories that have been proposed and to try to see what implications they might have for the future of life on earth. Although it must be emphasized that we have, as yet, no reason for suspecting that either of these ideas might be true, something even stranger could very well be. When scientific crises are encountered, it is sometimes the "crazy" ideas which have the best chance of turning out to be accurate.

One of the first ideas to be put forward was that something happened to the neutrinos which made it impossible to detect some of them. It has been known since 1962 that there are at least two different kinds of neutrinos. A pair of Soviet scientists suggested, therefore, that the neutrinos emitted by the sun might have a peculiar kind of "mixed identity" which would allow them to change from one type to the other and back again as they made their way from the sun to the earth. Since only half of the neutrinos reaching the earth would be of the variety which could interact with chlorine 37, the neutrino count would thus be lower than expected.

Most physicists do not take this idea very seriously. There is no independent evidence that neutrinos behave in such a way. Moreover, the idea would remove only part of the discrepancy between theory and experiment. Physicists maintain the same skepticism toward suggestions that some other fate might befall the solar neutrinos. They say that such ideas cannot be seriously considered until some confirmation is found in the laboratory; all the neutrino experiments that have been done so far seem to indicate that it is a very stable particle.

If the Soviet scientists' idea turned out to be true, however, it would "save" current theories of solar structure. If neutrinos could alter their identity, this would mean that there was something wrong with the physics that was used to predict a counting rate of 5 SNU. Astronomers would not be required to change their ideas, and it would be possible to assume that the sun was as stable as everyone had previously thought.

It is important to know whether or not the sun is stable. If, for example, the sun's energy output were to fall by only 5 per cent, the earth would become so cold that all the oceans would freeze, probably permanently. Since ice reflects most of the heat and light that falls on it, the oceans would not melt if the sun again became bright; they would continue to reflect most of the solar radiation back into space. There is no reason to think that anything like this will happen, but if something is not found wrong with current ideas about the physics of neutrinos, we cannot be sure that it is not possible.

According to another "crazy" idea, the observed neutrino count is low because the sun contains a black hole. According to this hypothesis, more than half the sun's luminosity is due, not to nuclear reactions, but to energy that is released by solar material falling into the black hole before it is crushed out of existence.

It is known that a black hole will "suck up" any matter that happens to stray into its vicinity. If this idea is accurate, then the sun is literally being eaten up. As the black hole consumes material, it will begin to grow at an ever-increasing rate. The more the hole grows, the faster the sun would disappear. Eventually, the solar system would have at its center not a bright star but a massive dark body with a temperature near absolute zero.

It is impossible to say how quickly all this would happen; it would depend upon how large the black hole had become at the present time. If it was large enough now to produce half of the solar luminosity, then the sun might have a billion or more years of life left. On the other hand, if the black hole was already so large as to account for most of the solar brightness, then the sun would undergo dramatic changes relatively soon. How soon, one cannot say: the theory has not yet been worked out in enough detail to be capable of making accurate predictions on this point. All one can say is that if there is a black hole in the sun and if it has already grown large, then the time that we have left is short compared to a billion years and long compared to the human life span.

A black hole would not have to destroy the sun completely before life became impossible on earth. As the hole sucked up more and more stellar material, greater amounts of energy would be released. The sun would become very hot as the process accelerated, and life on earth would be incinerated. The sun would again become cool as the black hole found its supplies of "fuel" to be dwindling. However, we would not be around to observe the process.

Needless to say, scientists remain as skeptical about this theory as they do about the theory of mixed-neutrino identity. It must be said, however, that this theory does seem capable of explaining a phenomenon with which conventional theories have never been able to come to terms.

We mentioned in Chapter 2 that there is, as yet, no completely adequate theory for explaining the formation of stars. The black hole theory does seem capable of describing this process. A tiny black hole, much smaller than a solar mass, could act as a "seed" and trigger the formation of a star. Interstellar gas would collect around it and contract in its gravitational pull. Before long, a very ordinary looking star would form. At first, while the black hole was very small, it would have little effect on the star's behavior. Billions of years would be required before it grew large enough to have any noticeable effects. One of the first of these effects, incidentally, would be a decrease in the number of solar neutrinos.

But all this is, at this point, nothing but speculation. All that can be said with any certainty is that the solar neutrino problem has not been solved, and, until it is, we will not be able to be sure whether or not the sun is a normal star and whether or not it is as stable as astronomers have always thought. Until we have an accepted explanation for Raymond Davis' neutrino experiment results, we cannot be absolutely certain that the sun will continue to behave in such a way as to allow the continuation of life on earth for any appreciable length of time.

5

ICE AGES

For the past 2 million years the earth has been in the grip of an ice age. During most of this period, mile-thick ice sheets have covered large areas of the Northern Hemispheres, sometimes as far south as the present location of Mexico City. Ice domes several miles in height have formed, and the regions we now know as Great Britain, Ireland, Canada, Denmark, Switzerland, and New Zealand have repeatedly been obliterated, while the United States, the Soviet Union, Mexico, Germany, China, and Australia have been threatened by widespread glaciation.

The glaciers have advanced more than twenty times. Each time they have ultimately retreated, until only the polar regions were covered with large sheets of ice. These warm *interglacials* have, however, been of relatively short duration. In most cases they have lasted no more than 10,000 years. The periods of glaciation, on the other hand, have gone on for more than 100,000.

The warm climate that we are presently experiencing must

therefore be considered abnormal. If, in the years to come, the earth's climate is anything like what it has been in the past, then we can expect only a brief respite. It appears fairly certain that human civilization will soon be threatened by advancing glaciers. It is impossible to tell when the next period of glaciation will begin. It will certainly happen within a thousand years; it could happen within our lifetimes. Scientists have already detected signs that the earth is cooling, and recent research seems to indicate that glaciation can be quite rapid, that massive ice sheets could form in the space of a few decades.

The term "ice age" has two different meanings. It can be used to refer to long periods during which glaciers alternately advance and retreat or it can mean a single episode of glaciation. So far, I have been using it in the first sense. In order to avoid confusion, however, it might be best to change our terminology. From now on, periods like the last 2 million years will be referred to as "ice epochs," and the term "ice age" will be reserved for individual periods of glaciation. In other words, we are living in the midst of a long ice *epoch*, at a time when a new ice *age* is about to begin.

Only a few decades ago it was commonly believed that we could look forward to a long period of uninterrupted warmth. If scientists were afraid of anything, it was that the large quantities of carbon dioxide released into the atmosphere by man's industrial activities might create a greenhouse effect that would cause temperatures on the surface of the earth to rise. The carbon dioxide, it was thought, would block infrared heat radiation that might otherwise escape into space. This could lead, in turn, to the melting of both polar ice caps, with a consequent rise in sea level and the inundation of cities located in coastal areas. The idea that a new ice age might be imminent hardly entered any reputable scientist's mind, for it was believed at the time that interglacial periods tended to be 100,000 to 275,000 years in length. Since the current interglacial was only 10,000 years old, it was thought that we could look forward to millennia of warm climate.

Scientific thinking on this subject has reversed itself in recent years. New methods have been developed which have provided us with a better understanding of the climatic history of the earth. Some of the old ideas about ice ages have been proved to be wrong, and it has become apparent that the next period of glaciation is much closer than had previously been thought. The carbon dioxide that has been poured into the atmosphere does not seem to have had any measurable effect on temperatures. It has become apparent that the earth is not warming at all; since 1950 it has been gradually growing cooler. If human industrial activities are having an effect at all, they are accelerating this process.

Every year the burning of fossil fuels releases billions of tons of carbon dioxide into the atmosphere. Although much of this carbon dioxide is dissolved in the oceans, that which remains in the air would act to warm the earth slightly, if it were not for the fact that other kinds of pollution seem to have the opposite effect.

Our industrial activities also produce large quantities of dust and smoke particles. Although the precise nature of the effects which this produces is still a matter of scientific controversy, it seems probable that the dust forms a kind of atmospheric veil which blocks out part of the sun's light, counteracting the effect of the carbon dioxide. As far as anyone can tell, man's activities have not had an effect on the average temperature of the earth at all.*

In 1972 a group of scientists met at Brown University for a conference entitled "The Present Interglacial, How and When Will It End?" They concluded that industrial pollu-

* Recently there has been renewed concern about increasing levels of carbon dioxide in the atmosphere. On the other hand, there are also new studies which indicate that destruction of forest lands could cause the earth to cool. Thus, since this chapter was written, uncertainties about the earth's future climate have become even greater.

tion seemed not to have had any discernible effects on the earth's climate. "The present climatic trends," they concluded, "appear to have entirely natural causes, and no firm evidence supports the opposite view."

This does not mean that human activities will not affect the climate in the future. It is possible that we might hasten the coming ice age or find ways to slow or reverse the glaciation once it begins. Although this subject is of some interest, a discussion of it will be put off until later. We have digressed long enough. It would be best, at this point, to take a closer look at what the current climatic trends are and to try to see why scientific thinking on the subject of ice ages has undergone such great changes in recent years.

It wasn't until the beginning of the nineteenth century that anyone began to suspect that glaciers had ever spread over wide areas in the past. At about this time geologists began to notice that Swiss valleys often contained rounded boulders composed of rock quite different from that which formed the valleys themselves. Since rocks like these had been seen along the sides of glaciers at higher elevations, they concluded that these glaciers must have once reached lower ground and have subsequently retreated to the mountains.

This idea was not hard to accept. As far as anyone knew, there had always been glaciers in the Swiss Alps. The idea that they might have once had a greater extent was not unreasonable. In 1837, however, the young Swiss naturalist Louis Agassiz went a step further and proposed an idea which seemed at the time to be quite outrageous. The ice, Agassiz said, had once stretched all the way from the Alps to the adjacent plains; even the low ground had once been covered by glaciers. Then, three years later, Agassiz announced that he had found evidence that ice sheets had once covered all of Great Britain.

At once, there was a storm of criticism. Agassiz's theory, older geologists suggested, was scientific heresy. Agassiz was a

The Horsehead Nebula, a region in Orion which contains large amounts of interstellar dust. (Photo courtesy of the Hale Observatories)

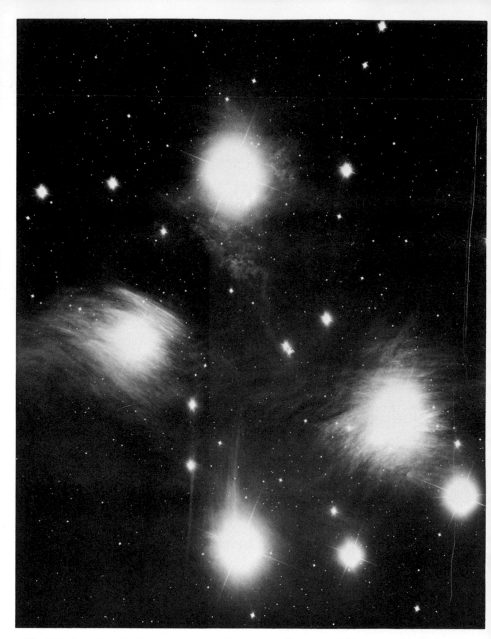

The Pleiades. These bright young stars in Taurus are still surrounded by interstellar dust, which produces the nebulosity apparent in the photograph. (Photo courtesy of the Hale Observatories)

The Crab Nebula in Taurus. The Crab Nebula comprises the remains of the supernova of A.D. 1054. After nearly a thousand years, the material which made up a massive star at its center is still hurtling outward into space. (Photo courtesy of the Hale Observatories)

The galaxy NGC 5236 photographed with and without a supernova. Although the supernova is a single exploding star, it appears almost as bright as the galaxy itself. (Photo courtesy of the Hale Observatories)

A *solar prominence 100,000 miles high. The sun is not a calm, evenly burning body: its surface (lower part of photograph) is quite turbulent. Many processes which take place both on its surface and in its interior are not yet completely understood. (Photo courtesy of the Hale Observatories)*

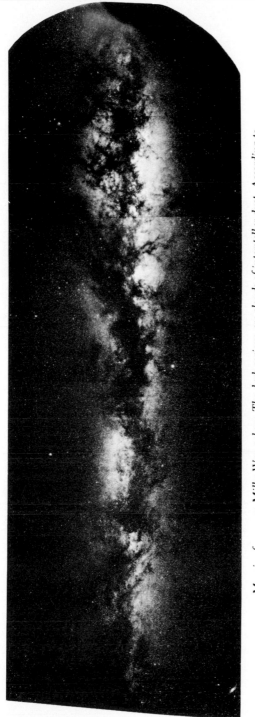

Mosaic of our own Milky Way galaxy. The dark regions are clouds of interstellar dust. According to one theory, ice ages are precipitated when the sun passes through just such a dusty region. (Photo courtesy of the Hale Observatories)

The galaxy in the center is a Seyfert-type galaxy. Seyferts are galaxies which seem to be undergoing enormous explosions in their cores. Although the source of the energy that is observed to be emitted is still a subject of scientific controversy, it is possible that such galaxies could contain massive central black holes. The energy released when matter falls into these black holes could account for their brilliance. (Photo courtesy of the Hale Observatories)

youthful and inexperienced observer, they charged; his findings were obviously ridiculous.

New scientific ideas often become accepted only as the older, more conservative, scientists retire or die. This is exactly what happened in the case of Agassiz's ice age theory. It was not accepted by the older generation, but as younger scientists with more open minds gradually replaced them in the universities, the theory became orthodox.

By the beginning of the twentieth century, it had been established, or so it was thought, that there had been four major ice ages. In 1906 two German geologists named them after four Swiss valleys: Günz, Mindel, Riss, and Würm. Although it was difficult to tell exactly how long the ice ages had lasted or to determine the length of the intervening warm periods, a rigid orthodoxy quickly grew up. Each of the ice ages had lasted around 100,000 years, scientists said, while the interglacials had been 125,000 to 275,000 years in length. Thinking on the subject became quite rigid. Where it had once been considered absurd to propose that there had been an ice epoch at all, any suggestion that there had been more or less than four major ice ages was now thought to be heresy. One was allowed to suggest, at most, that there might have been one or two additional minor glaciations.

Hindsight makes it seem obvious that the four-ice-age theory was built on very shaky foundations. When the glaciers spread, they stripped the soil from the earth and deposited it elsewhere, along with the rocks that had been gouged up. This provided abundant evidence that ice ages had taken place. But since each glaciation tended to obliterate the traces of the previous one to some extent, scientists should have realized that they could not be so confident either about the number of ice ages that they had discovered or of their duration.

It was not until the 1960s that new evidence began to accumulate which led to the overthrow of the orthodox theory.

Scientists began to drill into the ice sheets of Greenland and Antarctica, removing ice cores of up to 4,500 feet in length. Studying these cores enabled them to obtain data on climatic changes on the earth for periods of up to 150,000 years in the past. Cores were also extracted from ocean beds which provided data on climatic change over even longer periods. Studies of fossil pollens provided yet more evidence. Gradually a picture which was entirely at odds with the conventional theory began to emerge.

It became apparent that there had been eight major ice ages in the last 700,000 years, and a dozen or more previously. The warm interglacials had not lasted for as long a time as had been thought; on the contrary, they were relatively short. Furthermore, glaciation was not a process which took place gradually over periods of thousands of years; an ice age, it seemed, could get well under way in less than a century, possibly within a few decades.

Scientists also studied the climatic history of the earth during more recent times. Here, studies of tree rings supplemented the other methods. Samplings of rings from the bristlecone pine, a tree which can live more than 4,000 years, provided records dating 8,000 years into the past (the record could be extended back beyond the birth of living trees by matching their ring patterns against those found in older, dead stumps). It was found that the earth had been undergoing a slow cooling process for 6,000 to 7,000 years. Although a warming trend had been observed roughly from 1900 to 1950, this had been nothing more than a short interruption in the over-all pattern.

At this point a skeptic might object that one cannot be certain that the new theory is any more likely to stand up than the old one. If scientific fashions have changed before, he might ask, why cannot they change again? Such skepticism would be misplaced, for the new methods give us information about past climates which is much more reliable than the observations of rock scrapings that originally suggested the four-ice-age theory. At some point in the future, it might become necessary to make some minor modifications in the now accepted ideas, but it is very unlikely that there will be any major changes.

The new methods give scientists ways to "take the temperature" of the earth during bygone eras. To be sure, there can be some ambiguity when one applies the tree-ring technique. A wide ring can indicate either a wet year or a warm one, and narrow ones can imply periods either of drought or of cooling. The other methods, however, allow inferences to be made in a fairly straightforward way. For example, if fossil pollens are found in a layer of sediment that can be accurately dated, direct information about climate is obtained. Certain species of vegetation will flourish only in warm climates, while others thrive when it is cold. If one set of pollens is replaced by another, this furnishes evidence of a warming or a cooling trend at a certain point in time.

The cores extracted from ice sheets and from ocean beds can be used to make even more direct measurements of past temperatures. Both methods are based on the fact that oxygen is composed of two stable isotopes; it is 99.8 per cent oxygen 16 and 0.2 per cent oxygen 18 (there is also some oxygen 17, but the quantities are so small that its presence can be ignored). Oxygen 18, or O-18, is about 12 per cent heavier than the other, more common, isotope. Since a water molecule contains two atoms of hydrogen and one of oxygen, water made of O-18 will be slightly heavier than that containing the lighter isotope.

The lighter water molecules evaporate more readily. Furthermore, the difference in evaporation rates is correlated with temperature. When it is warm, more O-18 rises into the atmosphere, and when it is cold, most of it remains in the ocean. Since glaciers are formed from precipitation and since precipitation comes from evaporated water, measurements of the amount of O-18 in the various layers of a permanent ice sheet give a record of the earth's past climatic history. A large amount of O-18 indicates a period of relative warmth, while low levels of O-18 provide a record of periods of cold.

The cores taken from ocean beds give similar information, but here it is marine fossils that are studied, not the ocean sediment itself. Again, O-18 measurements are made, but this time everything works in reverse. There is more O-18 in the ocean (and hence in the fossils) when it is cold (because less has evaporated) and less O-18 when it is warm. It is therefore possible to reconstruct past temperatures in the seas as well as on land.

If it is possible to obtain accurate records of the earth's past climatic history, this does not imply that the causes of ice ages are well understood. In fact, they are not. The problem is not that there is any lack of theories; if anything, there are too many. It has been hypothesized that ice ages are brought on by changes in the earth's magnetic field, by sunspots, by wobbles in the earth's orbit, and by the dust ejected into the atmosphere by volcanoes. The blame has been put on variations in the energy output of the sun, on changes in deep currents in the ocean, and on variations in carbon dioxide distribution in the atmosphere. According to most theories, ice ages begin when the earth cools, but there is at least one theory which maintains that glaciation is initiated when the climate grows warmer. This is not as paradoxical as it sounds. A warming trend would cause more water to be evaporated from the ocean. This would, in turn, induce more precipitation; there would then be more snow in the colder areas of the earth. The additional snow would cause existing glaciers to grow. And, once the glaciation was well under way, the earth would become cold again.

Most climatologists doubt that ice ages begin in warm periods, but this has not prevented one scientist from combining this theory with speculation about the presumed effects of the passage of the sun through dust lanes in the spiral arms of the Milky Way galaxy. According to this theory, the sun becomes brighter when it passes through a galactic dust cloud. Its increased luminosity causes the earth to warm and glaciation to begin. This theory is anything but universally accepted. Some scientists, in fact, suggest that perhaps glaciation takes place not when the sun moves into a dust cloud but when it passes out of one.

It is also possible that ice ages could be precipitated by "ice surges" in the Antarctic. According to this theory, the Antarctic ice sheet will gradually increase in size over a period of thousands of years. When it becomes large and heavy enough, its weight will begin to melt the ice where it is in contact with the surface of the earth. This will cause large sections of the ice sheet to slide into the ocean. These sections will break up and drift northward, and there will be widespread cooling over the surface of the earth.

Altogether there have been more than fifty theories which have attempted to explain why ice ages begin. Some of these have been shown to be wrong, but there remains a large number that might possibly be correct. At this point, however, it is probably futile to attempt to make a choice beween them. Most likely, there is an element of truth in more than one. After all, there is no reason to believe that a single factor must cause the onset of glaciation; more probably, ice ages are due to the interaction of a number of different processes.

At one time it was believed that the onset of glaciation was a slow process. According to the old theories, glaciers expanded slowly, taking thousands of years to attain their full extent. They would never present any sudden threat to mankind, it was thought. If a glacier was seen to be expanding into a valley, for example, the area's present inhabitants could safely ignore it. Perhaps, hundreds of years in the future their descendants would have to move, but there would be no reason to worry in the immediate future.

Recent scientific research seems to indicate that the theories of glaciation on which such ideas were based are wrong. The beginning of an ice age is not a slow process; on the contrary, it is an extremely rapid one. If glaciers began to creep into one's valley (or into Chicago, or into New York), then, in all probability, the area would have to be abandoned within a dozen or so years. Once an ice age begins, it can be well under way in a matter of decades.

Ice age glaciers, we know now, do not expand horizontally; they build up vertically. As the earth's climate gradually grows colder, snowfalls begin earlier in the autumn and continue later in the spring. Sooner or later there will be a summer during which the snow that lies on the ground does not all melt. When winter comes again, the snow pack will increase. During the following year, there will be even more unmelted snow. If no warming trend reverses the process, a permanent ice sheet will cover the ground in a short time.

As ice sheets form, the rate of glaciation increases. Ice and snow, after all, reflect quite a bit of light. Up to 85 per cent of the solar radiation that falls on them is reflected back into space. Once it has extensive ice and snow cover, the earth absorbs less heat from the sun and the cooling process accelerates, plunging the earth ever deeper into an ice age.

It takes some time before the glaciation attains its full extent; mile-high ice sheets are not built up overnight. Large areas of human habitation will be threatened long before this happens, however. New York, for example, will be just as uninhabitable when it is covered by 150 feet of ice as it will be when it lies under a glacier a mile thick.

Since the causes of ice ages are not understood, it is impossible to predict when the next one will begin. This event will almost certainly happen sometime in the next thousand years, possibly in the next few hundred, or even before the end of the twentieth century. When the coming ice age does begin, large portions of the nations in the Northern Hemisphere will be covered by ice. Some of them will be obliterated entirely.

Even the countries in equatorial regions will feel the effects. Although it is not very likely that they will be covered by glaciers, they will experience prolonged drought. As the earth cools, less water will evaporate from the oceans. This will eventually bring a halt to the glaciation; there will be little water vapor in the atmosphere, and hence there will not be much snow to feed the glaciers. But before this happens, areas of the world which currently experience abundant rainfall will become very dry. In fact, something like this is already happening on a minor scale. The African drought that caused the death of 400,000 people during the late 1960s and early 1970s and which caused the Sahara Desert to creep southward is thought to be associated with the worldwide cooling trend that we are currently experiencing. Even before the next ice age starts, we can expect the summer monsoons that bring rain to large areas of Africa and Asia to fail repeatedly. It is not pleasant to speculate about the number of deaths that will probably result.

Although previous ice ages undoubtedly caused a certain amount of death and suffering, the disasters it created must have been of a local character. The last ice age ended 18,000 years ago, at a time when agriculture had not yet been invented and the human population was sparse. The population was thinly distributed over the earth in hunting–gathering societies, and it was still possible to migrate to warmer regions if the climate became too severe.

Today we are much more vulnerable. If an ice age was to begin now, it is probable that billions would die within a relatively short time. Paradoxically, it is our advanced technology that has created this vulnerability. Modern health measures and the development of high-yield hybrid grains (the so-called green revolution) have allowed us to increase our numbers beyond any reasonable bounds. Famines already take place even when the over-all climate remains good. If average temperatures continue to drop, the results will be disastrous. Croplands in some regions will be covered by ice and snow, and there will be drought in others. The deteriorating weather conditions will make it more difficult to ship surplus food (if there is any) to regions where it is needed. Since the new, high-yield grains have less genetic variability than the older varieties, they will be less able to adjust to the changing conditions. Crops will fail, and there may be less food than there would have been if the green revolution had never taken place.

The nations with the greatest population problems are frequently also the most unstable politically. In a worldwide crisis, this instability might become even worse. The leaders in some of the nations experiencing severe famine might very well decide to engage in "nuclear blackmail" by threatening to set off nuclear explosions in the major agricultural countries if their demands for food were not met.

(At present, six nations—the United States, the Soviet Union, Great Britain, France, China, and India—possess nuclear bombs or warheads. It has been estimated that another fifteen or twenty either have the technology required to make an atomic bomb or could develop it very quickly. It is true that only those nations with highly advanced technologies have the capability to develop sophisticated nuclear missile systems. However, it is not necessary to have ballistic missiles in order to engage in nuclear terrorism. An atomic bomb could easily be loaded into a Volkswagen bus and driven into New York City. A timing device could be attached which would cause it to explode at a given time if the blackmailers' demands were not met.)

The coming ice age, then, will cause the obliteration of millions of square miles of the earth's surface. It will bring drought and famine to those areas that are not covered by ice and provide motivation for possible acts of nuclear terrorism.

Is there any way that all this can be prevented? Perhaps. It might be possible to stop an ice age by melting the ice in the Arctic Ocean.

There are a number of ways in which we might attempt to do this. It should be possible to build a dam across the Bering Strait; warm water could then be pumped from the Pacific Ocean into the Arctic. Another method would be the spreading of coal dust or some other highly absorbing material over the Arctic ice. The dust would absorb more solar radiation than ice or snow. This would cause the arctic ice cap to melt over a period of years or decades. The melting of the ice would not cause any rise in sea level. Since there is no land immediately around the North Pole, the ice cap floats in the Arctic Ocean. When ice that is floating in water is melted, there is no increase in volume. Anyone who doubts this need only observe ice melting in a cocktail glass to be convinced.

The removal of the Arctic ice might cause the Greenland ice sheet to melt also and in turn cause the seas to rise 15 to 20 feet. This in itself would be no catastrophe, except perhaps in the Netherlands. However, it is impossible to predict what other changes might take place. In such a situation, we cannot be sure that they would not be serious ones.

Humanity does not have a very good record in the area of ecological tampering. Our attempts to make slight modifications in the balance of nature have repeatedly backfired. An attempt to modify the earth's climate in a major way could have unanticipated effects that were even more serious. We might successfully halt the glaciation only to discover that we were causing not only the ice in Greenland but also that in Antarctica to melt. In such an event, the oceans would rise not 15 but 150 feet. Coastal areas would be flooded, and the geography of our entire planet would be changed. Many of the world's major cities, such as New York, London, and Tokyo, would no longer exist.

It is even conceivable that melting the Arctic ice, or attempting to, could cause wild climatic fluctuations that would bring on an ice age more severe than any which we might otherwise have experienced. At present, we simply do not know enough about the mechanisms of climatic change to be able to predict what effects large-scale tampering might have.

If the next ice age is anything like previous ones, it will not bring about the end of the world. In the past, the glaciers have always eventually retreated, however far they have advanced. An ice age might cause the deaths of billions of people and destroy most of Western civilization. However, humanity and some of its technology would probably survive.

Provided, of course, that the entire earth does not freeze. It was noted previously that a 5 per cent decrease in the energy output of the sun would be sufficient to cause the freezing of the oceans. But if an ice age was already underway, if the earth was already cold, an even smaller drop in the sun's luminosity might have the same effect. If something like this happened, the ice covering the surface of the earth would reflect so much of the sun's radiation back into space that temperatures would drop permanently to approximately $-80°$ C (about $-110°$ F). The earth would become a frozen ball on which life was no longer possible.

Some other combination of factors could conceivably create the same result. The dust that we have ejected into the atmosphere seems to have had little or no cooling effect so far. We don't know, however, what the effects might be if the dust levels increased. Neither do we know what climatic effects other kinds of pollution may have. Hence we have no way of telling what would happen if natural causes somehow combined to produce an ice age of unusual severity and if human activities somehow managed to make it just a little worse than it would otherwise have been. Since we do know that an ice age is on the way, perhaps now is the time to start worrying about whether or not we are taking this kind of risk. It seems fairly reasonable to assume that nature has no intention of destroying the earth by covering it with ice. However, if it somehow happens to be prodded a little too far in that direction by human technology, we might find that this danger has suddenly become very real.

6

MASS EXTINCTIONS
IN THE FOSSIL RECORD

Dinosaurs became extinct approximately 70 million years ago. Although they were an extremely successful group of reptiles which had existed for as long as 200 million years, they suddenly disappeared from the face of the earth.

Scientists have suggested numerous explanations for the extinction of the dinosaurs. One, already noted in Chapter 3, is that they might have fallen victim to a nearby supernova. Another, somewhat more bizarre, theory is that the dinosaurs died because they were constipated. It seems that, at about the same time that the dinosaurs became extinct, flowering plants began to replace the gymnosperms, or naked-seed plants, that had previously flourished. The few gymnosperms which still exist often produce oils with strong purgative properties. The disappearance of most of these plants 70 million years ago, the theory says, would have denied the dinosaurs the natural laxatives upon which they had presumably learned to depend.

It is easy to laugh at such an idea. One doesn't often en-

counter sober scientific theories with such scatological character. But the theory is not taken seriously, not because it deals
with dinosaur droppings but because it explains so little.

The trouble with this hypothesis is that when the dinosaurs perished, they alone did not die. The fossil record provides evidence that quite a large number of species, including
both land and sea animals, disappeared at the same time.
Furthermore, there have been other, similar, episodes of mass
extinction. About 225 million years ago, for example, as
many as 40 per cent of the species then inhabiting the earth
seem to have died out. At other times, as many as a third of
the known species suddenly vanished. There is no question
about the reality of the extinctions. The paleontologists who
examine fossils found in sediments say that the sudden absence of previously abundant species is like night and day. It
is obvious that no theory which purports to provide us with
an explanation for the extinction of the dinosaurs can be considered adequate unless it also explains why millions of other
species have suddenly disappeared.

In 1963 Robert J. Uffen of the University of Western On-
tario suggested what seemed to be a plausible solution to this
baffling problem. Uffen pointed out that there have been
numerous periods, each several thousand years in length,
during which the earth's magnetic field was reduced to zero.
Since it is the magnetic field that shields us against incoming
cosmic rays, Uffen continued, it was possible that the extinctions could have been caused by high levels of radiation. This
radiation would produce mutation rates that were much
higher than normal, causing some species to die out.

It soon became apparent that there were difficulties with
the theory, at least in the form originally proposed. Calculations showed that the removal of the geomagnetic field
would not have any very great effect on radiation dosages.
Most of the cosmic rays would still be absorbed by the
earth's atmosphere; the increase would only be of the order

of 10 per cent. Furthermore, it was hard to see how cosmic rays could have any effect on marine life. Radiation does not penetrate very deeply into the ocean; at most, it affects only the layers within a few feet of the surface.

Uffen had, however, stumbled upon something that was very important. Although it did not seem likely that the cosmic-ray suggestion could be correct, there did seem to be strong evidence that the extinctions were related to variations in the magnetic field, more specifically to phenomena known as *magnetic reversals*.

The details of the generation of the earth's magnetic field are not completely understood. The field is believed to be caused by motions in the earth's molten iron-nickel core which are set up by variations in the earth's rotation. The field can have either of two possible orientations. Approximately half the time the north magnetic pole (the north pole according to compass readings) is very close to the true North Pole (as determined by the earth's rotation). The other half the time, the polarity of the earth's field is reversed; the north magnetic pole lies in the Southern Hemisphere, while the south magnetic pole is in the north. There is nothing paradoxical about this state of affairs; calling the two kinds of pole "north" and "south" is nothing more than a matter of linguistic convention.

Reversals of the magnetic field take place at irregular intervals. At times the field retains the same polarity for 50 million years or more; sometimes it will reverse itself after 100,000 years or fewer. The last reversal took place about 600,000 years ago. It has been established that there have been more than twenty reversals in the last 4.5 million years.

Reversals do not take place instantaneously. Before the magnetic field can change its polarity, it must be reduced in intensity. Reversals take place when the field decreases to about 20 per cent of its usual strength (not zero per cent, as Uffen believed). It remains at this weak level for 5,000 to

20,000 years before a field of opposite polarity is established. The biological extinctions are apparently a consequence of these long periods of low magnetic intensity.

No one is really sure what mechanisms cause the weakening of the field to affect life. However, the correlation is clear. Scientists working in the field called *paleomagnetism* have established beyond any doubt that magnetic reversals and the disappearance of animal species have frequently taken place at about the same time.

Paleomagnetism is the study of the geomagnetic field at various times in the past. All rocks in the earth exhibit magnetic properties. Many of them are found to have a magnetization which is referred to as *fossil magnetism* or *natural remanent magnetism* (commonly abbreviated to NRM). This remanent magnetism can arise in several ways. Lavas which erupt at temperatures of 1,000° C or more acquire, upon cooling, magnetizations in the direction of the earth's field. This magnetization is remarkably stable; one could say that it is "frozen in" the volcanic rock. Sediments also acquire NRM when they are formed, because the earth's field can align small particles in certain directions. Although rocks acquire other kinds of secondary magnetization, these are not as stable as the NRM. It is possible to remove these secondary magnetizations in the laboratory. The NRM can then be measured, and the direction and intensity of the earth's field at the time of the rock's formation can be inferred.

Since rocks exhibiting NRM can be dated by the same methods that paleontologists use to date rocks containing fossils, it is possible to tell when biological extinctions take place in close proximity to field reversals. Up to a point, that is. Sometimes the evidence is conclusive, and sometimes it is not: some extinctions were more abrupt than others, and there are uncertainties in dating. The farther one goes back in time, the greater these uncertainties become. Hence it is only possible to say that the extinctions often coincided with reversals. It is not likely that we will ever know for sure whether or not they always did.

In particular, the extinction of the dinosaurs is one of those that has not been conclusively correlated with one particular magnetic reversal. Several reversals did take place at approximately the right time, but the uncertainties in dating are such that the demise of the dinosaurs might be related to any of them, or to none. The question of what it was that brought the Age of Reptiles to an end is therefore still unanswered. A magnetic reversal is only one of several plausible possibilities.

Despite this, there exist numerous theories which try to explain the presumed biological effects of weakened magnetic fields. The simplest suggestion is that weakened fields affect life directly. However, few experiments have been performed to determine the effects of magnetic fields weaker than the normal field of the earth. There is some evidence that reduced fields can induce behavioral and biochemical abnormalities, but it cannot yet be considered conclusive.

Bacteria kept in a weak magnetic field seem to suffer a significant reduction in their reproduction rate. Other studies have indicated that the behavior of flatworms, protozoans, mollusks, and birds can be affected, while mice exhibit significant changes in enzyme activity and a shortened life span. The effects of low magnetic fields are, according to one experimenter, "potentially lethal."

But scientists hesitate to accept such results until the experiments have been repeated a number of times and it has been shown that no unknown cause has influenced the results. Furthermore, it is not yet known how magnetism might affect life, although two explanations have been offered. One is that magnetic fields align biological molecules in certain directions, affecting the complex biochemical processes that take place within the body. The other is that there might be interactions between the magnetic fields and charged ions in cell membranes.

Until someone is able to demonstrate conclusively that magnetism does affect life in one of these two ways (or in some other way), the theory is not likely to be generally accepted. Scientists do not like to accept theories that depend on the existence of hypothetical mechanisms for which there is no evidence. Since—as we shall see—there are a number of indirect ways in which magnetism might have an effect on life, the question is still an open one.

One suggestion is that changes in the earth's magnetic field affect climate. While the idea that magnetism is associated with climatic change is not an implausible one—the geomagnetic field does provide a shield against certain types of solar radiation, and increased radiation could modify climate—it is difficult to see how these climatic changes could cause the death of so many organisms. The earth would presumably be the warmest when the field intensity was low; the cold periods would occur between magnetic reversals, not during them. Furthermore, temperatures would change much more slowly in the ocean than they would on land. It is hard to see how magnetically induced climatic change could affect both terrestrial and marine organisms in the same way.

Yet another hypothesis links the biological extinctions to solar activity. According to this theory, the earth's magnetic field protects us against energetic particles coming from the sun. When the geomagnetic field is in its normal state, it will deflect these particles, preventing them from reaching the surface of the earth. But when the field is low, they will enter the atmosphere, giving rise to processes that have profound effects on life.

In the late 1950s, satellite experiments showed that there was a steady stream of protons and electrons coming from the sun. They were speeding past the earth at a velocity of about 400 kilometers per second (about 900,000 miles per hour). The reason they had not been observed before the advent of space vehicles was that the earth's magnetic field caused them to follow paths that curved around it. Although some were trapped in the Van Allen radiation belt, few ever made their way to the earth's surface; scientists simply did not see them.

This stream of particles is known as the *solar wind*. At the earth's distance from the sun, there is a flux of 500 million particles per square centimeter per second. It is the solar wind that produces the auroras which are seen in the high northern and southern latitudes and that pushes comet tails away from the sun. If the solar wind did not exist, life on earth would not be possible, for it tends to sweep cosmic ray particles out of the solar system and thus drastically reduces the radiation levels on the earth's surface. The earth's atmosphere and magnetic field could not block it all out. The solar wind removes hydrogen (the protons and electrons that fly past the earth are dissociated hydrogen) from the sun at a rate of about a million tons per second. Yet this has no significant effect on the sun's mass; during the next 5 billion years the sun will lose less than one hundredth of 1 per cent of its mass in this manner.

Although the solar wind helps to protect us from cosmic rays, it can become less benign when the earth's magnetic field is weakened by a reversal. To be sure, there are no immediate effects; the atmosphere continues to protect us from the effects of the incoming solar particles. The solar protons, however, might induce the formation of nitrogen oxides in the atmosphere. As we already know, these oxides can cause a partial destruction of the ozone layer. As a result, some of the lethal ultraviolet radiation that is normally blocked by the ozone will reach the earth's surface.

If the solar wind were all we had to contend with, there would be little cause for worry. Enough ozone would remain so that the increase in ultraviolet radiation would have few significant effects. If a magnetic field reversal took place today, these effects would make us more susceptible to sunburn, and the incidence of skin cancer would increase. Skin cancer is not, however, one of the leading causes of death; most types are not very serious. And, in any event, clothing would provide adequate protection.

All this has, however, suggested yet another theory which attempts to explain how magnetic field reversals might be connected with biological extinctions. Of all the ideas advanced to date, this one, which concerns itself with the effects of *solar flares*, is one of the more plausible.

Solar flares are vast explosions on the sun's surface which produce streams of particles that are much more intense than those associated with the solar wind. A single flare can cause the number of protons entering the atmosphere to increase by a factor of 10 or more.

If the sun is especially active during a field reversal, flares could cause the ozone layer to be utterly depleted. Ultraviolet radiation would then become so intense that exposure to sunlight would be fatal to humans. We would not be able to go outdoors without protective suits, and mutation rates would increase in all organisms, both animal and plant, that were exposed to sunlight.

It must be emphasized that this scenario is a very speculative one—it is difficult to calculate exactly how strong or numerous the flares would have to be to remove the ozone, and we do not really know what the probability is that the sun will be especially active during any given magnetic reversal. The ozone does have the ability to replenish itself, so conditions on earth depend very much on how close together the flares are.

Astronomical observations tell us how active the sun is now, but we do not know whether there were a greater or lesser number of flares in the past, and we can only guess how many there will be in the future. It may be that the sun has been relatively active during the short time that astronomers have been able to look at events on its surface, or it may be in an unusually inactive state. Since the sun's activity could presumably vary according to cycles that were hundreds, thousands, or even millions of years in length, we must conclude that we have almost no data concerning what its "normal" state might be. The solar-flare theory must therefore also be considered unproven.

The evidence that biological extinctions *are* associated with magnetic field reversals is conclusive. It is not known, however, whether these extinctions are caused by induced climatic changes, by biomagnetic effects, by solar flares, or by some as yet unknown effect. And, of course, the extinctions might be due to some combination of two or more of these factors.

In spite of our lack of an adequate theory, we can be reasonably certain that future reversals of the earth's magnetic field will present a significant danger to the human race. Even if no deleterious effects accompany the next reversal, we would still have reason to fear the succeeding one, or the one after that. We do know that at least during some reversals large numbers of organisms die.

The next reversal could take place fairly soon. The magnetic field of the earth has been decreasing for more than a century now. Since 1835, the year in which the German mathematician Karl Friedrich Gauss made the first detailed measurements, it has weakened by about 6 per cent. No one is certain whether or not this trend will continue. We may be experiencing nothing more than a temporary fluctuation. On the other hand, a reversal might take place sooner than we think. If the strength of the magnetic field continues to decline at its present rate, the zero point will be reached in about two thousand years. If it begins to weaken at an increasing rate, a reversal could happen much sooner.

A magnetic field reversal could turn out to be especially dangerous to human life. Since no one is sure about the nature of the dangers that we would face, it would be difficult to prepare for them. We might work out ways to protect ourselves against ultraviolet radiation or reduced magnetic fields, only to discover that the real culprit was some other effect.

The life that has evolved on our planet is remarkably resilient. Since the first living organisms sprang into existence over 3 billion years ago, there have been nearby supernova explosions, magnetic field reversals, large-scale climatic changes, and, probably, variations in the luminosity of the sun. In spite of all this, life has not only survived, it has also continued to evolve. It seems virtually certain, therefore, that living organisms will continue to inhabit the surface of the earth until some point billions of years in the future when the sun becomes too hot to support life as we know it.

But life similar to man, or intelligent life of any kind for that matter, may not continue to exist as long as that. Human intelligence is nothing more than the latest in a long series of evolutionary experiments, and it has not yet proved to be an especially successful one. *Homo erectus* came on the scene only about 2 million years ago, after all. The dinosaurs ruled the earth for 200 million.

It could even turn out that man's highly developed brain could make him more vulnerable to the high radiation levels that are associated with many of the possible cosmic disasters than other, less intelligent, species. Radiation, after all, induces genetic mutations. If these affected us to a greater extent than other creatures, our present evolutionary edge might be rapidly transformed into an evolutionary disadvantage.

The suggestion that I am making is, admittedly, a speculative one; however, I don't think that it is unreasonable. I see no reason why mutations might not affect the most complex organ that we possess, our brain, in such a way that our continued survival becomes unlikely. I don't mean that radiation is going to turn us all into psychotics; there is no evidence that anything like that can happen. What I want to suggest is that there might be harmful mutations which would affect our behavior in less dramatic but still meaningful ways.

In recent years it has been shown that somewhat more of man's behavior is genetically programmed than had previously been thought. This suggests that mutations which spread throughout the species during periods of high radiation levels could conceivably affect our nervous systems in such a way as to interfere with behavior that was conducive to survival.

What would happen if we became just a little more aggressive or a little more irrational? Some authors—Arthur Koestler, for example—suggest that man is already mad. What would the effects be if we grew just a little crazier than we already are?

It must be pointed out that there are no *known* mutations which affect behavior and also that high dosages of radiation do not induce any mutations which do not occur naturally. It only increases their frequency. It is known, however, that predisposition toward certain types of mental disease is hereditary. It is not unreasonable to suppose that these predispositions might eventually be shown to be caused by mutated genes.

One does not often encounter neurotic lions or disturbed cockroaches. The so-called lower forms of life seem to be less vulnerable to malfunctions of the central nervous system than we are. When conditions become such, as they inevitably will, that the struggle for survival becomes much more difficult than it is at present, this fact may give other species the edge that they need. It is possible that they might survive while we perish.

To state categorically that having complex brains would prove to be a disadvantage under certain conditions would be going a bit too far, but we have no right to assume that the human brain must necessarily, in all conceivable circumstances, provide the advantages that it has in the past. Many species have died out because they could not adapt to new conditions. Although man is, at present, the most adaptable animal known, it does not follow that he will always be able to adapt better than any other. Nature is not yet finished with its evolutionary experiments.

7

COLLISIONS WITH
ASTRONOMICAL BODIES

A common science fiction theme has been that of an astronomical collision, of one kind or another, that would destroy the earth. Sometimes a star would collide with the solar system, sometimes a planet or a comet hit the earth.

We know now that, at least in one sense, these tales are not so farfetched as they might seem. The earth has suffered numerous collisions in the past, and it will experience many more in the future. The destruction, however, will probably be less than total. The collisions which could destroy our planet seem to be extremely unlikely. On the other hand, those which are likely to happen would allow life to go on, even though they might cause extreme devastation over certain areas of the earth.

There are a couple of possibilities which can be dismissed at once. The earth is not going to collide with Mars or Venus, and it is not going to fall into the sun. Planetary orbits are extremely stable; an enormous amount of energy would be required to change them to any significant extent, and we know of no natural process that could supply this energy. It is true that gravitational perturbations can cause small orbital changes, but this is a slow process. If, for example, the gravitational pull of the planet Jupiter disrupted the motion of Mars, billions of years would be required before this could conceivably cause any significant changes. Even then it is not likely that these changes would create any great danger to the earth.

Similar arguments indicate that a collision with another star is also unlikely. Stars move in orbits about the center of the galaxy, and it is equally unlikely that any of these will be suddenly disrupted. Furthermore, stars are very widely spaced; even if they moved randomly, collisions would take place only once every few hundred billion years.

Galaxies can and do collide with one another. Astronomers have observed such collisions taking place. However, such collisions are not especially catastrophic events. If the Milky Way were to intersect another galaxy like it, the two would simply pass through one another. Again, the wide separation of the stars would make destructive occurrences improbable.

However, if the other galaxy were not like our own, if it were made up of *antimatter*, there would be something to worry about. An encounter with an antimatter galaxy could cause the annihilation of millions of stars. In such a case, it might not matter whether or not our sun was one of them; even if it was not, the energy released in annihilations elsewhere would be quite sufficient to destroy all life on earth. It is possible to make some guesses about the likelihood of such an event, but first it will be necessary to say a few things about the nature of antimatter and its presence in the universe.

Every known subatomic particle has an *antiparticle*. The antiparticle of the proton is the *antiproton*, that of the neutron is the *antineutron*. The counterpart of the electron is the *positron* (it would be more consistent to call it an "antielectron"; however, the positron was discovered and named before any comprehensive theory of antiparticles existed). There are also antineutrinos, antiquarks, and even such strange beasts as anti sigma hyperons.

Antiparticles can combine in atoms the same way ordinary particles do. For example, hydrogen is made up of a proton and an electron. An atom of antihydrogen would consist of an antiproton and a positron. Similarly, we could have anticarbon, antioxygen, antinitrogen, and so on. Antimatter and matter are mirror images of one another.* In fact, the prefix "anti" is nothing more than a linguistic convention; matter and antimatter behave in the same ways. Since we are made up of matter ourselves, we apply the term "anti" to the variety which is unlike us.

Matter and antimatter cannot exist in conjunction with each other; when they come into contact there is mutual annihilation. The energy released in the mutual destruction is enormous. In a hydrogen bomb explosion about seven tenths of 1 per cent of the mass of the hydrogen is converted into energy. But when matter and antimatter collide, all the mass is destroyed and transformed into energy. A matter-antimatter explosion can therefore be said to be nearly 150 times as powerful as that of an H-bomb.

It is entirely possible that whole galaxies may be composed of antimatter. It is true that there is not yet any evidence that antimatter galaxies exist, but such evidence would be difficult to obtain. Matter and antimatter would look alike from a distance, and we cannot send probes into other galaxies and then watch to see whether or not they explode.

There are theoretical arguments which seem to indicate that matter and antimatter should exist in equal amounts in the universe, but no one knows how valid these arguments

---

* The more mathematically inclined should, perhaps, be warned that the author does not mean to imply anything about reflection symmetry here; "mirror image" is used only as metaphor.

are. All that can be said with any certainty is that antimatter
is rare in our region of space. When galaxies collide, matter-
antimatter explosions are not observed to take place.

This does not mean that antimatter galaxies will not eventually be discovered. For all we know, the nearby Andromeda
galaxy could be made up of antimatter, and it could conceivably collide with our own galaxy some day, destroying it in the
process. If such an event was to take place, however, it would
lie billions of years in the future, long after the earth had been
vaporized by the sun. One must conclude that destruction by
antimatter is yet another possibility that we can safely discount.

However, the same cannot be said of collisions with black
holes. Since we do not know how many black holes there are,
it is impossible to calculate the probability of an encounter
with one.

It is believed that black holes are formed when stars that
are much more massive than the sun undergo gravitational
collapse. If the star is massive enough, gravitational forces
will crush its matter out of existence once its nuclear fires die,
producing a dark object that neither gives nor reflects light.

An encounter with such a black hole would be no more
likely and no more destructive than a collision with another
star. In fact, since a black hole emits no radiation, it could
pass closer to us than a star could without creating any ad-
verse effects. A black hole will suck up any matter that happens to approach near enough, but so will any gravitating
body. All in all, such black holes cannot be said to present
any very significant threat.

It is possible, however, that not all black holes are relics of
dead stars. Some astrophysicists think that the universe might
contain billions of "mini black holes." Theoretical calculations indicate that black holes of this variety could have been
formed shortly after the big bang that marked the beginning
of the universe. Since the matter density was still very great

at the time, enough mass might have been compressed together here and there to form these small black holes. If such objects exist, they would come in varying sizes: some would be no larger than a virus but would weigh millions of tons; others might be the size of dust particles and weigh trillions of tons or more.

If a mini black hole happened to strike the earth, it is unlikely that any worldwide cataclysm would result. It would simply pass through our planet, doing no more than some local devastation at the points where it entered and left. If it entered the earth through one of the oceans and left through another, it might not even have any very noticeable effects.

However, according to British physicist Stephen Hawking there is a mechanism by which mini black holes could spontaneously explode. If Hawking's ideas are correct, such black-hole disintegrations could release energy equivalent to that of as much as a billion 1-megaton H-bombs. If such an explosion took place near the earth, life could be brought to an end in an instant.

It may be that mini black holes do not exist. At the moment there are only theoretical reasons for believing in them; there has, as yet, been no experimental confirmation. But if mini black holes are real, there could be millions of them in our solar system. If such turned out to be the case, we would have to learn to live with the knowledge that we were surrounded by miniature time bombs capable of producing massive explosions that could destroy us at any moment.

If the earth lasts long enough, it may eventually collide with fragments of its own moon. Although it is likely that our planet will suffer some other fate first—such as vaporization by the red giant sun—the breakup of the moon remains a possibility if, for some reason, events proceed faster than we think they will.

It has been known at least since the time of Sir Isaac Newton that gravitational force exerted by the moon is responsible for the high and low tides of the earth's oceans. Those parts of the sea that are directly under the moon are pulled upward, while those on the opposite side of the earth, which are subjected to a weaker pull, bulge in the opposite direction (which also turns out to be upward; this explains why there are two high tides per day). The moon also produces tidal effects in the atmosphere and in the earth's crust. Land areas will rise several inches or more when the moon is overhead.

The earth-moon system possesses a certain amount of energy. Some of this energy is dissipated by a process called *tidal friction*. The rate of the earth's rotation is therefore gradually slowing, while the moon slips into orbits that are progressively farther away.

Now these effects are not large. At present, the slowing of the earth is only enough to increase the length of the day at about the rate of a thousandth of a second per century, and the changes in the moon's motion are hardly discernible. The changes will, however, continue to take place until the month and the day are equal in length. At that time the earth will always keep the same face toward a distant moon (provided, of course, that the earth and moon still exist), and the day will be about a thousand hours in length. When this point is reached, there will be no more tidal friction and energy dissipation will cease.

Both the earth and the moon will, however, still be subject to the tidal action of the sun, which will cause the earth's rotation to slow still more, while the moon begins to approach the earth again. The moon will come closer and closer until its distance from the earth reaches a certain critical figure called *Roche's limit*—about 10,000 miles from the earth. When this happens, the gravitational action of the earth will cause the moon to burst apart. Some of the fragments will rain down on the earth's surface, while others will form rings similar to those of Saturn.

There is still much that is not understood about the dissipation of tidal energy, so we cannot say exactly when all this will happen. The time required might be of the order of tens of billions of years. In that case, the breakup of the moon is something that will never happen. The destruction of the moon in this manner is, barring the unlikely event that gravitational perturbations exerted by other astronomical bodies will somehow accelerate the process, something that we probably need not worry about. Some other catastrophe is certain to destroy the earth first.

If collisions with other stars or planets are extremely unlikely, collisions with comets are not: every time a comet crosses the earth's orbit, there is one chance in 500 million that it will hit the earth. Since there are about five such comets per year, cometary collisions should take place about once every 100 million years, but they arc probably not very destructive. The heads of comets seem to consist of numbers of small fragments, most of which would burn up in the earth's atmosphere. To be sure, some comets are quite large. Although it probably isn't quite cricket to compare the size of a spherical body to an area on the surface of the earth, it might not be too misleading to say that the biggest comets are about the size of the state of Vermont. Even comets of this size probably do not pose any great threat.

The last collision with a comet may have taken place as recently as 1908. In that year an enormous explosion took place in the Tunguska region of the Central Siberian Plateau. A gigantic pillar of fire shot into the sky; it was visible hundreds of miles away. Trees were knocked down within a 50 mile radius, and the noise was so great that it could be heard at distances of up to 500 miles. Thick clouds rose into the atmosphere to a height of 12 miles. But because the area was so sparsely populated, there were no known human deaths.

Nineteen-eight was a year of great political upheaval in Russia, and it was not until 1921 that a scientific expedition set out to study the site of the explosion. It became apparent at once that the blast could not have been caused by a meteorite; there was no crater. Today the most widely accepted theory is that the explosion was caused by a collision with a comet that disintegrated before it reached the surface of the earth.

But it has not been conclusively demonstrated that it was a comet which caused the 1908 event, and other theories abound. It has been suggested, for example, that a piece of antimatter might have hit the earth. A collision with a mini black hole is another suggestion. The black hole might have emerged in an ocean on the other side of the earth. According to yet another hypothesis, the explosion was nuclear. This would imply, of course, that an alien spaceship was somehow responsible. Our extraterrestrial visitors, according to this theory, might have detonated a bomb for some unknown reason or possibly their ship exploded.

Asteroids strike the earth much more frequently than comets, about once every 250,000 years or so. Such collisions are also much more devastating; asteroids produce craters up to 20 kilometers (about 12 miles) in diameter and release energy equivalent to that of 10,000 10-megaton H-bombs.

The moon, Mercury, Venus, and Mars are covered with craters that are the product of such collisions. The earth is also covered with such craters, but until rather recently no one realized that they were there: on earth the traces of such a crater are obliterated in less than 600 million years, and of course there is no crater at all when the asteroid falls into the ocean.

The craters are, therefore, hard to find. In recent years, however, close inspection of aerial photographs has revealed faint traces of some, and subsequent geological study of the sites has unearthed evidence that collisions with asteroids have indeed taken place there.

The bodies with which the earth collides are not members

of the main asteroid belt between Mars and Jupiter, but rather bodies called *Apollo objects*, which have elongated orbits that cut across the path of the earth. Some of them pass very close to the sun; many follow paths that make it possible for them to collide with Mercury, Venus, and Mars as well as the earth and the moon. The name "Apollo object" is a reference to the first such body to be discovered by astronomers, the asteroid Apollo, which was discovered in 1932.

It is not known exactly how many Apollo objects there are. Since, by astronomical standards, they are very small, they are difficult to locate. Even though extensive astronomical searches have been going on for some time, only about four new Apollos are found every year. It is estimated that the total number is between seven hundred fifty and a thousand.

Since about four of these strike the earth every million years and many others collide with the moon and with other planets, there would not be any Apollo objects left at all if there were not some means to replenish the supply. It seems likely that most of them come originally from the main asteroid belt, although others might be extinct comets that have been "outgassed" by repeated approaches to the sun.

The mechanisms which cause members of the asteroid belt to move into new orbits are complicated. It is safe to say, however, that the planet Jupiter is the main culprit. The gravitational influence of Jupiter and, to a lesser extent, that of Saturn, can create perturbations which cause asteroid orbits to become elongated. If they become elongated enough, some of the asteroids will make close approaches to Mars. A number of such approaches in succession will induce additional perturbations which will alter an asteroid's orbit still more, turning it into an Apollo object.

The entire process could take less than 100 million years. Unfortunately, calculations seem to indicate that such a process does not produce enough new Apollo objects to keep their total number constant. The perturbations produce one new Apollo every million years; in the same time, fifteen will collide with our moon or with one of the four inner planets.

This present existence of large numbers of Apollo objects is the main reason some astronomers believe that some of them must be dead comets. Since asteroids produce large craters while comets probably do not, comets would have to undergo changes before they could be classed with the asteroids. However, there seems to be no reason why they should not do just this. When a comet approaches the sun, it will be heated and volatile substances will boil away into space. Once this outgassing process is complete, a comet could presumably coalesce into a solid object.

The procedure by which a comet might become an Apollo object is even more complicated than that which draws bodies out of the main asteroid belt, but once again Jupiter plays the most important role.

Cometary orbits are subject to the same gravitational perturbations that affect other astronomical bodies. They will be affected by the gravitational pull of any planet to which the comet makes a close approach. Since Jupiter is by far the largest planet (its mass is more than twice that of all the other planets combined), it is this body that will have the greatest influence. Ejection of gas and dust from a comet can also play a role if the comet is rotating on its axis. Although the process by which this would induce orbital changes appears complicated, there is nothing more involved than Newton's law of action and reaction.

Finally, it has been suggested that collisions within the asteroid belt itself could eject asteroids and turn them into Apollo objects. It seems very unlikely, however, that many new Apollos are produced in this manner. The energy required to eject an asteroid from the belt is so great that any collision capable of sending one into an earth-crossing orbit would be likely to shatter it into a number of small fragments.

There have been no collisions between the earth and an Apollo object in modern history. The most recent such encounter took place somewhere between 25,000 and 50,000 years ago, when an object struck the earth, forming the well-known Meteor Crater in Arizona. This crater is only about 4,000 feet in diameter; the asteroid that created it must therefore have been of a relatively small size. It is not known when the most recent impact of a larger body with the earth took place; possibly its traces have already eroded away.

Close encounters with Apollo objects happen relatively frequently. In 1937 the asteroid Hermes passed within 485,000 miles of the earth, or about twice the distance to the moon. And in 1968 Icarus missed the earth by 4 million miles, a distance that is much larger, but still small by astronomical standards. Such encounters will take place many times before an asteroid actually hits us, but one will certainly do so.

It is impossible to predict when this will happen. The majority of the Apollo objects have not yet been located by astronomers, and others have been lost for long periods of time. Anything as small as an asteroid is hard to find and hard to keep track of. Hence, when an impact does become imminent, it is not certain that we will have any advance warning.

Although the devastation will be great near the point of impact, life and civilization will certainly go on. The worst thing that could happen would be to have an Apollo object fall in the ocean. This would create enormous tidal waves which would be likely to engulf most of the coastal areas of the world. An impact on land would, at worst, destroy an area the size of California or eastern New England.

While an astronomical collision seems one of the most obvious ways that the world could be brought to an end, an examination of the evidence forces us to conclude that it is really not a very likely one. The collisions that could destroy us are so unlikely to occur that they can be discounted, while those which will take place will cause destruction that is less than total. It is true that the end could be brought about by a large hunk of antimatter or a mini black hole that happened to be lurking in our vicinity, but there is, as yet, no conclusive evidence that either of these exists. One must conclude regretfully that, in this instance, the science fiction writers have misled us. Having something ram itself into the earth is not, after all, a very likely way to bring everything to an end.

8

MAN-MADE
CATASTROPHES

Escherichia coli, a species of bacteria which inhabits the human intestinal tract and which helps us to digest our food, is one of the most promiscuous creatures known; its potential for sexual activity is probably unequaled by any other living organism. Although *E. coli* normally divides once every twenty minutes or so, it often neglects the business of reproduction for up to two or three hours while it engages in sex. Or, in other words, the sex act can be prolonged to around nine times its normal life span. *E. coli* is indiscriminate in its tastes; male bacteria will mate with females, with other males, and even with other species. It has been observed to perform the conjugal act with members of more than twenty different genera.

Sex does not have the same function in bacteria that it has in higher organisms. It is not related to reproduction, but rather to the transfer of genetic material. For this reason, many biologists prefer to refer to it not as "sex" but as *con-*

jugation. But, whatever term we use, the similarities between it and mammalian sex are striking.

Bacteria carry most of their genetic information in a single chromosome made up of a long chain of DNA. Some of them also contain small, independently replicating bits of DNA called *plasmids.* When plasmids are present in an *E. coli* bacteria, the organisms will grow threadlike tubes called *pili,* which are equivalent in function to the mammalian penis. The possession of a pilus is the factor that confers "maleness" on a bacterium; it can use the appendage to inject plasmids into other organisms. Since the plasmids replicate during conjugation, the male bacteria is able to transfer genetic information while retaining the plasmid itself.

The ability to transfer genetic information contained in plasmids is the factor that makes bacterial evolution so rapid. In higher organisms, mutations can be passed on only to the descendants of the animal possessing the mutated gene. In bacteria, mutations can be transferred by the process of conjugation to members of the same or other species. It is the transfer of plasmids, for example, that has conferred resistance to antibiotics on so many different bacterial strains.

E. coli was, until fairly recently, thought of only as a harmless inhabitant of the intestinal tracts of animals. However, in the last decade or so, a number of pathogenic *E. coli* strains have been discovered, and *E. coli* has been associated with various kinds of diarrheal diseases, with blood poisoning, and with urinary infections. *E. coli*'s promiscuity has been responsible for the creation of other problems as well. This once-harmless human symbiont has been implicated in the evolution of penicillin-resistant strains of gonorrhea, for example. It has been shown that resistance to the drug comes from *E. coli* plasmids which were transferred to gonococci by conjugation.

Twenty years ago *E. coli* caused few medical problems. Plasmids were relatively rare, as were virulent strains of the bacterium. Today 30 to 50 per cent of all *E. coli* strains harbor plasmids. Although biological technology has grown more sophisticated and plasmids have become easier to detect, it is obvious that *E. coli* has undergone significant evolutionary change.

It is indubitably our environmental tampering that has caused these changes. The use of antibiotics as additives in cattle and poultry feed has certainly created selection pressures that have been responsible for some evolutionary modification of *E. coli*. Also, increased levels of water pollution has enhanced *E. coli*'s opportunity to exchange genetic material with other species.

Although *E. coli* is responsible for a growing number of deaths, it has not yet become a major threat to human life. But the medical problems that have resulted from its advances do provide a frightening illustration of the fact that man's technological activities can have deleterious effects that are impossible to foresee.

More often than not, these effects become noticeable only after it is too late to do anything about them. For example, the cancers caused by exposure to substances such as asbestos or to the various chemical components of air pollution appear not at the time of exposure but decades later. Since new technological processes are being introduced continually, it is likely that we are today creating new hazards which we will not recognize for years to come.

The creation of biological hazards is not always accidental; sometimes it is the result of deliberate tampering with genetics. In order to feed the world's growing population, we have created numerous hybrid grains with high productive yield, and more food can now be produced per acre than would have been thought possible a few decades ago. However, by increasing our dependence on "improved" varieties of crop plants, we have created a very real danger. Our hybrid crops have had their genetic variability bred out of them,

causing a serious depletion of the gene pool. Since it is genetic variability that gives plants the ability to adapt to new
diseases and to changing climatic conditions, we may be well
on our way to disaster.

In 1970, 20 per cent of the corn crop in the United States
was lost to blight; the genes that might have given the corn
resistance to the disease had been lost. It is not hard to imagine circumstances in which problems of this sort could become much worse. It is entirely possible that a new type of
fungus or a new bacterial disease could destroy a crop entirely. If the crop thus attacked happened to be a staple food
for a large region of the world, we could experience famine
on a scale never before known.

The more we tamper with the genetic content of agricultural plants, the more likely such a prospect becomes. At present, however, we may not have much choice. The world's
population has increased to such an extent that to go back to
the old crop varieties would cause hundreds of millions of
deaths. Population growth and technology have truly combined to make us vulnerable to the whims of nature.

Of all the possible biological threats, it is those which have
been posed by experiments with recombinant DNA which
have received the greatest amount of publicity. Strict controls
have been placed on such experimentation because of the
fear that scientists could unwittingly create new strains of virulent bacteria against which man—or some of the plants or
animals upon which he depends for food—would have little
resistance.

Are such dangers real? Probably not. But no one is really
certain that they can be entirely discounted. In any event,
there is still much that is not understood about biological
processes and about the genetic code. Since what we do not
know can create more potential harm than that which is well
understood, there are good reasons for placing stringent controls upon genetic experimentation.

Most recombinant DNA experiments involve the insertion of DNA from other organisms into *E. coli* plasmids. Even though weakened strains of *E. coli* that could probably not survive for long outside the laboratory are used, there remains the possibility that some sort of new plague could be created that could infect a large portion of the human race if the disease-carrying *E. coli* somehow managed to escape from the laboratory.

It might seem that since *E. coli* does inhabit the digestive tracts of man and of other animals, selecting it for use in genetic experiments is an odd choice. But more is known about the genetic makeup of *E. coli* than that of any other bacterium. Using a microorganism that is not a human symbiont would be possible, but this would delay research for a decade or more while the substitute bacterium was subjected to intensive study. Furthermore, there is no guarantee that this would reduce the danger. It is our lack of knowledge in certain areas, after all, that can produce the greatest dangers. It is probable that, if a biological monster was created, it would at least be recognized more quickly in *E. coli* than it would in some less familiar organism.

Recombinant techniques are extremely simple. Any type of DNA can be combined with any other kind with the help of *restriction enzymes* that have been isolated from bacteria. Restriction enzymes are chemicals which bacteria use to protect themselves from attack by other organisms—viruses, for example—by breaking up the DNA of the invader. Since the enzymes will act on any DNA, they can readily be used to split up DNA molecules in the laboratory.

The enzymes break the DNA into pieces that have "sticky" ends. The DNA pieces can thus be shuffled and rejoined. It is perfectly possible to combine human DNA with that of a potato or to join DNA from a chicken with that of a giraffe. However, the recombined DNA will not function unless it can somehow be inserted into a living cell.

This is where the *E. coli* comes in. If a cut is made in the DNA of an *E. coli* plasmid and a piece of foreign DNA is inserted between the broken ends, the recombined plasmid can then be inserted into a living bacterium. The net result is that the bacterium now contains an extra gene or genes taken from a foreign organism. When the *E. coli* divides, the daughter cells will contain the foreign gene also.

There are great potential benefits that might result from such experiments. Not only do they add to our store of knowledge concerning genetic processes, but there is also the possibility that they will produce significant advances in medical technology. One often-mentioned example is the commercial production of insulin, required by diabetics. If the gene which is responsible for the production of human insulin could be inserted into *E. coli* and somehow be made to function there, we would have a cheap, plentiful commercial supply of the drug. At present, the demand is threatening to outrun the supply, and diabetics sometimes have allergic reactions to insulin manufactured from animal sources.

At the moment, insulin production is no more than an intriguing possibility; there is no known method for identifying and extracting the insulin gene from a mass of human DNA. And if this does become possible, scientists may not be able to find any way to make the gene function inside an *E. coli*.

Foreign genes generally do not function when they are placed in bacterial cells. This is the reason recombinant DNA research has not yet yielded many practical results. It is also one of the reasons many scientists remain skeptical about the possible dangers of genetic research.

The belief that the hazards associated with genetic research are largely imaginary could, paradoxically, present the greatest danger of all. As the Three Mile Island nuclear power plant accident in Pennsylvania demonstrated in 1979, disasters that scientists think impossible or highly improbable can happen. Unforeseen events do occur, and supposedly stringent safeguards do break down. When scientists become complacent, disasters are more likely, for it is when we believe that there is no danger that we become the most careless.

At the Fort Detrick, Maryland, U. S. Army Research Laboratory there is a maximum-safety center at which work is done with known biological pathogens. Although safeguards have been made as stringent as possible and although hazards are known to be very real, dangerous viruses have escaped from containment: during the last twenty-five years, there have been 423 infections and three deaths there. In one of the more bizarre incidents, someone inadvertently picked up an aerosol can containing plague and sprayed a laboratory with it.

In 1978 simple carelessness caused a death from smallpox only a very short time after the World Health Organization announced that the disease had been eliminated from the earth. The victim was Janet Parker, a forty-year-old medical photographer at Birmingham University Medical School in England. An investigation revealed that Mrs. Parker had been infected by a virus from the laboratory. At the same time it became apparent that she would never have caught the disease had it not been for the fact that safety codes had been flagrantly violated.

At the moment, it does not seem very likely that organisms containing recombinant DNA are likely to pose any great threat to mankind, but one hesitates to imagine what might happen if a highly virulent, highly contagious organism were created and if safety procedures happened to break down at just the wrong moment.

If the possibility that biological hazards will arise from genetic research is still hypothetical, our technological activities have created other dangers that are very real. For instance, it has already become evident that pollution of the atmosphere is causing the ozone layer to become seriously depleted. It has been estimated that within fifty years the quantity of ozone will have decreased by as much as 15 per cent. Since this will cause a 30 per cent increase in the amount of ultraviolet radiation reaching the earth, we can reasonably expect that there will be significant biological effects.

One thing that we can look forward to is a significant increase in the incidence of skin cancer. But this is likely to be the least of our worries. Human beings will be able to shield themselves against ultraviolet radiation by wearing protective clothing and by spending less time outdoors; plants and animals that must remain out in the sun will not be able to do so. Although it is impossible to tell exactly what the over-all effects of increased ultraviolet radiation will be, there is no doubt that they will be significant. At the very least we should expect widespread ecological disturbances.

DNA, the biochemical substance most essential to life, is also the most vulnerable to ultraviolet radiation damage. Although there are biological mechanisms for repairing damage done to DNA by ultraviolet radiation, the balance is often precarious. When the intensity of ultraviolet radiation increases, the repair mechanisms in many species might be overwhelmed.

Ultraviolet radiation is especially likely to affect plankton in the ocean. Since plankton lies at the bottom of the food chain, a decrease in its abundance would in turn affect all other marine life. Although no one can tell what form they might take, ecological disturbances affecting terrestrial life might also arise from this.

Agricultural plants are also significantly affected by high levels of ultraviolet radiation. Experiments have shown that higher than normal levels cause significantly decreased yields in corn, peas, tomatoes, cotton, rice, soybeans, and lettuce, among other crops. The effects would not end with a decrease in our food supply. Water, oxygen, carbon dioxide, nitrogen, and sulfur are recycled through biological systems. If damage to plants interfered with these processes, there could be far-reaching effects, the precise nature of which is as yet unknown.

It is impossible to state in any very precise manner just what the effects of an increase in ultraviolet radiation will be because much of the necessary research on this topic has not yet been done. It wasn't until the mid-1970s that scientists began to realize that the ozone layer was being depleted. They only then began to theorize about the ways in which this will alter conditions on the surface of the earth. We know that we are going to have to make some major adjustments, but it is not yet possible to say exactly what these will be.

The possibility also exists that ozone depletion will affect the earth's climate, but again there is little that can be predicted with any degree of certainty. A 15 per cent ozone reduction will cause a 10°C rise in the temperature of the upper stratosphere. What implications this has for the climate at the earth's surface is uncertain. All that can be said is that it might have some effect on weather patterns, or it might not. We can only wait and see.

Ozone, or O_3, is a form of oxygen, its molecules containing three oxygen atoms. Ozone acts as a protective shield around the earth because it absorbs radiation so strongly; it blocks out a large wavelength range of the solar ultraviolet completely, preventing it from reaching the ground. Ozone is not as chemically stable as ordinary oxygen gas, or O_2, and quite a few chemical reactions can cause it to break up. Ozone is constantly being created, so all the ozone molecules which are destroyed naturally are ordinarily replaced, with the result that the concentration in the atmosphere remains fairly constant. Or at least it did, until man began to release substances into the atmosphere which caused ozone levels to decrease.

The atmosphere contains only a small amount of ozone—not more than 1 part in 100,000. Most of it is concentrated in the upper part of the stratosphere, about 19 miles above the surface of the earth. When chemical pollutants make their way to this height, they can cause a substantial depletion in the ozone by chemical reaction.

At present, most of the ozone depletion is being caused by fluorocarbons (also called "chlorofluorocarbons" or "halocarbons") which are used in aerosol sprays. Although the further manufacture of fluorocarbons for use as nonessential aerosol propellants was banned in the United States in December 1978, the ban covers only about a quarter of the world production. Even if man stopped releasing fluorocarbons into the atmosphere today, ozone depletion would continue for decades. Once fluorocarbons enter the atmosphere, they stay there; there are no significant processes that destroy them. Over a period of years or decades, they slowly diffuse into the stratosphere, where they are broken up by solar radiation. It is this breaking up which allows them to affect the ozone, for when they dissociate, chlorine is formed. Chlorine is one of the substances that can react chemically with ozone, causing it to be destroyed.

In recent years it has become apparent that the ozone problem is more serious than had previously been thought. In 1976 it was calculated that ozone depletion caused by the aerosols already present in the air would eventually reach 7 per cent. In 1978 this figure was revised upward to 15 per cent.* It is entirely possible that the estimate may be pushed upward again if it is discovered that other atmospheric pollutants are also having a significant effect.

One substance that might be doing just this is methyl chloroform, a chemical used in solvents, that is becoming present in the atmosphere in ever higher concentrations. It has been estimated that atmospheric methyl chloroform has a ten-year life-span, and that 10 to 15 per cent rises to the stratosphere.

* New studies indicate that the eventual depletion may be even higher, perhaps as much as 30 per cent.

Although it does not have as significant an effect on ozone as the fluorocarbons, it is responsible for some depletion, and since fluorocarbons already seem destined to nibble away 15 per cent, we certainly cannot afford to release chemicals that will make the problem even worse.

Ozone is constantly being created and destroyed, but before there were any fluorocarbons in the atmosphere, its concentration remained relatively constant because the two processes were in equilibrium; as many O_3 molecules were formed as broke apart. When fluorocarbons began to have an effect, the ozone level decreased. Eventually, a new equilibrium level will be reached. In fifty or a hundred years there will still be fluorocarbons in the air, but there will be less ozone to be destroyed and the depletion will halt. If the fluorocarbons suddenly disappeared, the ozone concentration would return to the previous levels.

But if we release chemicals into the air that interfere with the ability of the atmosphere to form ozone in the first place, the effects would be much more serious. The ozone layer could disappear completely. Unfortunately, it is not known whether or not something of this sort might even now be happening. Atmospheric chemistry is very complicated; scientists have come nowhere near reaching a complete understanding of it. Little is known about the effects of many of the gases that we allow to be released into the air, and not much more is known about the processes by which the atmosphere cleanses itself of ozone-threatening substances; we can only hope that we are not interfering with these in one way or another.

None of the phenomena considered so far in this chapter—
E. *coli* mutations, hypothetical new diseases that might attack hybrid crops, biological hazards resulting from DNA experiments, depletion of atmospheric ozone—is likely to bring the end of civilization or to cause the end of human life, at

least not by itself. Although we will certainly have to make some significant adjustments, our technology should be able to cope with the problems that have appeared so far.

But the prospect of having to go through great technological contortions in order to meet threats that technology itself has created is not very pleasant. And we seem to be reaching the point where before we can even decide what steps must be taken to protect ourselves against one danger, a new one appears. We can have every expectation that new threats to life in the biosphere will be perceived in the decades ahead. It is impossible to say what these will be. In recent years scientists have been discovering how much they do *not* know about atmospheric chemistry, about the mechanisms that govern climate, about the effects of the chemicals we are pouring into our air and water, and about the effects of ultraviolet radiation on life.

Despite our widespread concern about the ecological effects of our activities, we are doing little to avert the dangers. Although pollution controls have been imposed on many industries and environmental-impact studies are now commonplace, technology is still accelerating and energy consumption is increasing every year. New chemicals are developed and allowed to enter the biosphere in increasing amounts. It is certain that new crises will appear at an ever-increasing rate in the years ahead. Sooner or later we will encounter one that is so severe that we cannot cope with it. This crisis, whatever it may be, is not likely to have any single cause; it seems more probable that it will come about because of cumulative effects. For example, the climatic effects of the cutting down of forests in the Amazon basin could be reinforced by those arising from the presence of atmospheric dust. Water pollution might cause processes which interact with climatic change brought about by pollution of the atmosphere. Or, as we have already pointed out, ozone de-

The Great Galaxy in Andromeda. Of all the spiral galaxies, Andromeda is the nearest to the Milky Way. The light from it is shifting toward the blue, not the red, showing that it is approaching us. The Andromeda galaxy is an exception to the rule that the galaxies seem to be receding; it and the Milky Way are gravitationally bound. (Photo courtesy of the Hale Observatories)

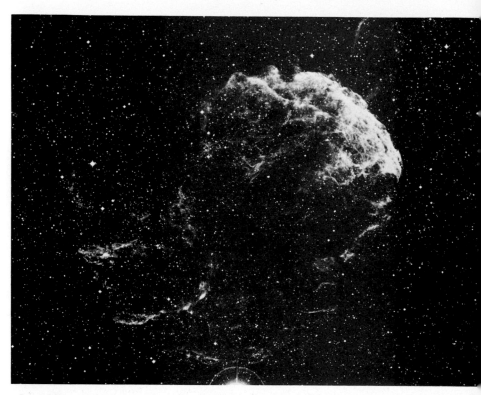

Interstellar gas appears in many forms. When it exists in a galaxy, it is relatively easy to see, for it is illuminated by nearby stars. Intergalactic gas, on the other hand, is very difficult to detect, for there are very few stars between galaxies. These two photographs depict the gaseous nebula in Gemini, ABOVE. *and the Lagoon Nebula,* OPPOSITE. *in Sagittarius. The latter also contains some dust. (Photos courtesy of the Hale Observatories)*

The nebulosity in Monoceros, another constellation in which new stars are being born. However, as entropy increases, sources of disequilibrium will disappear; there will no longer be sufficient gas and dust to make new stars. (Photo courtesy of the Hale Observatories)

The solar corona, photographed during an eclipse. The sun's atmosphere, or corona, which is heated to a temperature of 1 million degrees, is the source of solar-wind particles. (Photo courtesy of the Hale Observatories)

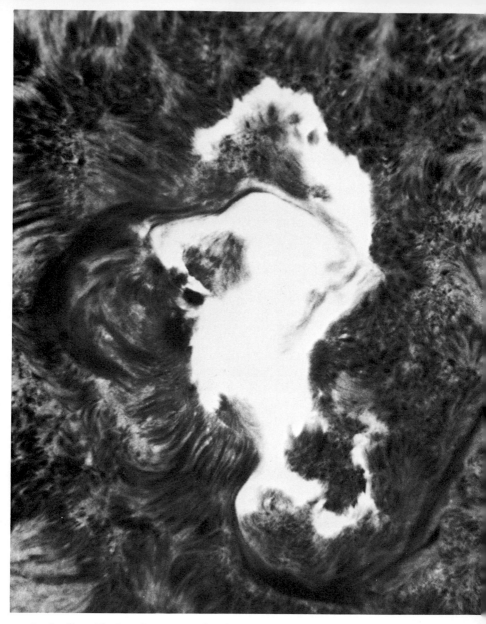

A solar flare. The hot white area in this photograph of a section of the sun's surface is a flare. Flares produce large numbers of energetic subatomic particles. Normally, most of these are deflected by the earth's magnetic field or absorbed by the ozone layer. During magnetic field reversals, however, many of them reach the earth's surface. (Photo courtesy of the Hale Observatories)

ABOVE, *two galaxies in
collision in the constellation Corvus.
Since stars in galaxies are so widely
spaced, such collisions are
not especially
catastrophic events.
(Photo courtesy of the
Hale Observatories)*

LEFT, *the Mrkos comet.
According to one theory, some
of the asteroids called "Apollo objects"
are outgased comets.
(Photo courtesy of the
Hale Observatories)*

Lunar craters. Collisions with asteroids create similar craters on the earth, but their traces erode away in a relatively short time. (Photo courtesy of the Hale Observatories)

struction might be reinforced by factors which prevent the ozone from being formed in the first place.

There is also a danger that human activities might make natural disasters much worse than they would otherwise be. An ice age is already coming; we could conceivably make it more intense. If a magnetic field reversal takes place at a time when ozone levels are already low, its effects would be especially severe. It is obvious that we cannot afford to continue to engage in environmental tampering on anything like the scale that we are at present.

If we are not to be the agents of our own destruction, we must learn to make do with a more limited technology. The myths concerning the dragon of chaos contain lessons that we have ignored too long. Soon we will have to realize that if we continue to heap insults upon Mother Earth, she is going to give birth to a monster much more fearsome than the one which nearly destroyed the Greek god Zeus.

So far, I have neglected the possibility that we may destroy ourselves deliberately. So much has been written on the possibility of a nuclear holocaust that there really isn't much to add, but I must point out that a visitor from one of the other advanced civilizations that might exist elsewhere in our galaxy would certainly think us mad when he perceived that we possessed nuclear weapons programmed to bring planetwide destruction at any moment.

In spite of the fact that there is a United Nations-approved nuclear nonproliferation treaty, nuclear weapons are being developed by nations that never possessed them before. As the number of bombs increases, it becomes more certain that, sooner or later, some of them are going to be used. Our only hope is that the destruction will be of relatively limited extent.

It is conceivable that even more destructive weapons might become possible. Nearly two decades ago Herman Kahn, in his book *On Thermonuclear War*, suggested the possibility of a "doomsday machine." Such a device would function as the ultimate deterrent, for it would destroy our entire planet if set off.

At that time, no one had any ideas as to how a doomsday machine might be constructed. However, since Kahn's book appeared, scientific knowledge has "progressed" to such a degree that the idea is not the fantasy that it once seemed. For example, it might someday become possible to capture or construct a mini black hole. If anyone wanted to destroy the world, it would only be necessary to drop such a black hole on the ground. The black hole would make its way to the center of the earth, simultaneously gobbling up matter and releasing energy. But, unlike a black hole that struck the earth with a high velocity, it would not emerge on the other side of our planet and move off into space. Instead, it would bob back and forth within the earth like a pendulum. As it did, it would grow larger and release increasing amounts of energy. It is impossible to say how long this would go on before the earth was blown apart or disintegrated. It is clear, however, that our planet would be destroyed.

It is easy to imagine circumstances under which such a device could be used. One possible scenario might run as follows. Climatic conditions deteriorate to the point where there are widespread famines. A large, underdeveloped nation that is especially hard hit decides to engage in nuclear blackmail. This nation possesses a doomsday machine as well as nuclear weapons, so it simultaneously demands large shipments of food from other nations and threatens to use the doomsday machine if any attempts are made to withold the shipments. One of the nations being blackmailed decides to call the bluff; it refuses to ship food and, after one of its largest cities is destroyed by the blackmailer's H-bombs, it launches a retaliatory nuclear strike. The threats of a doomsday machine turn out not to have been a bluff after all. . . .

II
THE END
OF THE UNIVERSE

9

THE DEATH OF THE STARS

Before they die, stars evolve into red giants. Some, the smaller ones, subsequently shrink to something less than their former size and die in a relatively peaceful manner. But the larger ones end their lives in a more violent way; they undergo supernova explosions. Because they are massive, they possess large reserves of gravitational energy which they can use to ignite the higher-order nuclear reactions which cause a star to explode. Some red giants, then, shrink and fade away, while others become supernovae. Although the two phenomena seem quite different, they are both caused by the exhaustion of nuclear fuel in the core of the star.

Red giants and supernovae, however, do not represent the final stages in the lives of stars. All stars are eventually transformed into *black dwarfs, neutron stars,* (see below) or black holes. Although there are obvious differences between the states which represent the end points of stellar evolution, there are many ways in which they are alike. Black dwarfs, neutron stars, and black holes are all tiny bodies which are highly compressed and which emit little or no heat and light. We can't always be sure which of these any given star will evolve into, but we can be certain that it will eventually go out. It is possible to say that every star is destined to become a cold, dark body of one kind or another.

As long as the nuclear reactions in the core of a star continue, heat energy and radiation pressure are able to support the outer layers. But when a star runs out of fuel, this is no longer possible and the star begins to undergo gravitational collapse. The more massive a star, the more powerful this gravitational contraction becomes. Large stars, therefore, compress themselves into denser objects than light ones. If a star is massive enough, it may reach the ultimate condensed state. Its matter will be crushed out of existence and it will become a black hole.

A star with a mass less than 1.4 times that of the sun will turn into a white dwarf. As it contracts from the red-giant stage, it may undergo some explosions or eject mass in various ways. However, nothing can stop the process of collapse; condensation continues over a period of the order of tens of millions of years, until the star becomes so dense that a tablespoon of stellar material weighs several tons.

At this point, condensation stops. The electrons, which make up most of the volume of the star's atoms, become so tightly packed together that further contraction is impossible. The electron *degeneracy pressure* holds up the dying star.

A white dwarf is roughly the size of the earth, or about one millionth the volume of the sun. Since a dwarf has no nuclear fuel left to burn, it is relatively dim. However, it can be quite hot. During the contraction process, large amounts of gravitational energy are converted into heat. This heat allows a dwarf to shine dimly for billions of years.

As a white dwarf cools, its color changes, just as a white-hot piece of iron becomes yellow, then red, then black as its temperature decreases. In a star, however, the process is much slower. Current theories about cooling rates and estimates of the age of the universe would seem to indicate that there has not yet been enough time for any white dwarfs to become completely black. It is unlikely that any have yet cooled to temperatures less than a few thousand degrees.

White dwarfs are quite numerous, indicating that the universe has existed long enough for billions of stars to be born and die. Since the universe is likely to last tens of billions of years longer, if it does not go on forever, we can be sure that the time will come when cold black dwarfs are the most populous objects in the sky.

The first white dwarf to be discovered was Sirius B, the companion of the bright star Sirius. Although Sirius B was first observed in 1862, it wasn't until 1914 that the American astronomer Walter S. Adams calculated its size. When he did, most scientists refused to accept his results. They could not believe that any star could be made up of matter that had been compressed to a density a million times that of terrestrial rock. It wasn't until 1926, when the British mathematician R. H. Fowler worked out a successful theoretical model for white dwarf stars that Adams' results began to be accepted.

The enormous density of white dwarfs was only the first of the surprises that were in store for astronomers. They soon began to realize that it was possible for even more highly condensed objects to exist. In 1934 the American astronomers Walter Baade and Fritz Zwicky performed some theoretical calculations in an attempt to see what would happen to a dying star of 1½ or 2 solar masses. They found that electron degeneracy pressure would not be sufficient to stop the contraction; the gravitational forces would become so strong that the electrons would be crushed into the atomic nuclei. The negatively charged electrons and the positively charged protons would be squeezed together to form neutrons. The electron degeneracy pressure would disappear, and the star would contract still further until the neutrons were packed together as the electrons had been in the white dwarf stage. At this point the collapse would stop; the star would now be held up by neutron degeneracy pressure.

In 1939 the American physicist J. Robert Oppenheimer and his student George Volkoff worked out Baade's and Zwicky's ideas in more detail, demonstrating that the idea that neutron stars might exist was an entirely reasonable one. For the next few decades, however, their work was ignored. No one really knew what a neutron star—a body a billion times as dense as a white dwarf—might look like or how it could be observed. A neutron star would have a diameter about equal to the length of Manhattan Island, or about 13½ miles. Could such an object actually be seen?

The first neutron star was finally discovered in 1967. Like many important scientific discoveries, it was accidental. At Cambridge University, the British radio astronomers Jocelyn Bell and Antony Hewish had set up equipment designed to detect radio emission from the stars. It was their intention to make an attempt to measure the size of various galactic radio sources. They found a neutron star instead.

It was during the summer of 1967 that Bell first noticed something odd about some of the data that the radio telescope was producing. Pulses of radio emission were being detected at about the same time every night. At first she thought that the cause might be interference from some source on earth. Radar installations, electric motors, and other devices can create static in radio telescopes just as they do in radio and television receivers.

But by September it became apparent that the cause was extraterrestrial. Measurements made two months later showed that pulses 0.016 seconds in duration were arriving every 1.33730115 seconds. Before long, other sources of pulsed radio emission were also discovered.

It was at about this point that some of the scientists began jokingly to call their radio sources "LGMs" (for "Little Green Men"). No one seriously believed that contact had been made with an extraterrestrial civilization, for the pulses were too simple in nature; they contained little or no information. This, however, did not prevent the *National Enquirer* from reporting that scientists had discovered an extraterrestrial civilization.

During the following year, 1968, the solution to the problem was worked out. One of the sources of pulsed radio emission was found to lie in the middle of the Crab Nebula, the remnant of the supernova of A.D. 1054. The pulsing radio source, or *pulsar*, was a small body that had been formed during or after the 1054 explosion. Since the Crab Nebula pulsar produced 30 pulses per second, it had to be spinning very rapidly. The Cambridge astronomers concluded, therefore, that it must be a neutron star; nothing else could rotate with the necessary velocity without flying apart.

Today no one doubts that this conclusion was correct, that pulsars are indeed neutron stars which emit radio waves (and sometimes light) in a manner similar to the beacon in a lighthouse. As a pulsar rotates, its beam sweeps by at regular intervals. Astronomers are not quite sure how the beams are produced. It is thought that neutron stars have magnetic fields which cause charged particles to be emitted in certain directions. These particles are presumably responsible for the radio emission, but the details of the process have not yet been worked out by theorists.

Some neutron stars are associated with supernova remnants. It follows that neutron stars can be formed in the aftermath of a supernova explosion. It is not known whether or not all neutron stars are associated with supernovae. Scientists know only that a neutron star is formed from a star that is too big to become a white dwarf. It is estimated that a star of more than 1.4 solar masses will become a neutron star, but this does not tell us how big such a star was originally, since

an object called Cygnus X-1, a strong emitter of X-rays in the constellation Cygnus.

Many star systems are binary; unlike our solar system, which has only one sun, they are made up of pairs of stars which revolve around one another. In certain cases, we can infer the presence of a black hole from its effects on its companion. Theory tells us that X-rays should be emitted in large quantities when matter from the visible star is drawn off by the black hole.

Cygnus X-1, a binary system consisting of a supergiant star with an invisible companion, seems to fit this theoretical description. Calculations indicate that the X-rays could be produced in the observed quantities only if the invisible object is a black hole.

But it is not possible to be absolutely certain. Some astronomers have pointed out that the visible star might have two dark companions, neither of which is a black hole, and that this could conceivably account for the X-ray production. Although this seems unlikely, the fact that such an alternate explanation can be proposed forces us to conclude that although the existence of black holes is very probable, it has not been established beyond doubt.

Some popular writers have called black holes "cannibals" which gobble up any matter that strays into their path. While this description is reasonably accurate, it does create a misleading impression. A black hole really does not differ from any other gravitating body in this respect. The earth, for example, gathers up a lot of material as it travels through space, small objects which are observed as meteors.

A black hole does not possess any mysterious properties that would allow it to gather in appreciably more matter than any other body of the same mass. Individual black holes of stellar mass do not, then, constitute any great danger to the earth, to the galaxy, or to the universe. They are not cosmic vacuum cleaners which go around gobbling up stars and planets.

Unfortunately, the same cannot be said of the black-hole "superstars" which some astronomers think might exist in galactic cores. Stars are packed close together in the centers of galaxies, and if very large black holes form there, the situation could be quite different.

Our sun occupies a position near the rim of the Milky Way, and the stars that occupy this region tend to lie rather far apart. The one that is nearest to us, for example, is more than four light-years away. In the galactic core, on the other hand, the average distance between stars is only a fraction of a light-year. Large black holes that form there might eventually devour all matter in their vicinity.

In time, such black holes could grow to the equivalent of millions of solar masses. The larger they got, the faster they would "eat" up the surrounding matter. In time, entire galaxies could be converted into black holes. It is true that this process might take tens of billions of years, but once it started, there might be nothing that could stop it.

To be sure, some stars would survive because they were located far from galactic centers, but they in turn would eventually become black dwarfs, neutron stars, or black holes themselves. All the stars are fated to die eventually, in one way or another.

Astronomers are not certain that these massive super black holes do exist in galactic cores; at the moment the idea is still speculation. The existence of such objects would explain a lot, however. Numerous galaxies have been observed to be undergoing gigantic explosions. Until black holes were discovered, there were few good ideas to explain what the energy sources could be, but now there is at least a plausible explanation. A super black hole could cause the release of enormous quantities of energy by drawing material from sur-

rounding stars in a manner similar to the way that the hypothetical black hole in Cygnus draws matter from its stellar
companion.

In recent years there has been quite a bit of speculation
concerning the possibility of traveling into black holes. The
idea is not as crazy as it may seem. It is true that anything
that entered a nonrotating black hole would be crushed out
of existence. But spinning black holes are a different matter
entirely. Theory appears to indicate that it might be possible
for a space vehicle to enter such a black hole and to emerge
again in a different region of space.

It must be emphasized that such ideas are speculative.
There does not exist any experimental evidence that black
holes might function as interstellar gateways similar to the
"space warps" that have so frequently been used by science
fiction writers. The idea emerges quite naturally from the
mathematics that is used to describe black-hole structure.
However, as every physicist is aware, mathematical theories
sometimes produce "unphysical" results that have no counterpart in reality.

Furthermore, there are theoretical arguments which pur-
port to show that if such gateways did open, they would close
themselves off immediately. In such a case no spaceship
would ever have any opportunity to pass through them. If
these arguments are valid (at this point it really isn't possible
to tell whether they are or not), then the gateways could be
considered to have no more than an odd, somewhat meta-
physical, sort of existence. If something disappears at almost
the instant that it is created, it is hard to put it to practical
use. It is true that modern physics is full of such evanescent
entities. Some of the elementary particles have lifespans that
are only small fractions of a billionth of a second, yet they
are considered to be quite "real." A black-hole gateway, however, would have to be there long enough to allow something

to pass through it in order to exist in any meaningful sense of the term.

If the gateways do exist, we cannot tell where they might lead. A space vehicle that traveled through one of them might find itself in a different, "parallel," universe, or in our own universe at a moment billions of years in the past. The latter possibility suggests that if it is possible to enter black holes and survive, then time travel might be possible. It is true that travel into the past could create paradoxes that would imply violations of causality, but then perhaps our belief in causality is only a philosophical prejudice. The only thing that is known with reasonable certainty is that travelers into black holes would not be able to return to the here and now; they would be embarking on one-way journeys.

Since we cannot see into black holes, we would have no way of knowing whether or not the travelers even survived. There are reasons why they might not. Enormous tidal forces exist in and around black holes, with gravitational fields so strong and so incompatible that an astronaut falling feet first into a black hole might be stretched into a long thin thread. Since his feet would be nearer the singularity at the center of the black hole, where its mass is concentrated, than his head would be, there would be more gravitational attraction on them; they would be drawn downward with much more force than the other end of his body.

This possibility, incidentally, led to an amusing exchange between a Soviet and an American scientist during a 1972 symposium on communication with extraterrestrial intelligence. The following is a quotation from the transcript of the meeting. The dialogue began when N. S. Kardashev of the Soviet Institute for Cosmic Research made some rather complacent comments about black-hole travel. He was immediately challenged by the Austrian-born astronomer Thomas Gold of Cornell University's Center for Radiophysics and Space Research.

KARDASHEV: The tidal stress depends upon the dimensions of the body relative to the gravitational radius. Such estimates have been made and everything seems to be quite satisfactory.

GOLD: I thought if the radius was only two kilometers or so, the stresses would be very large and a human being would certainly be drawn into a long, thin thread.

KARDASHEV: Of course, but only for a very short time, you must remember.

GOLD: I don't wish to be a long thread even for a very brief moment.

Such ideas about black-hole travel have more relevance to the theme of this book than they might seem, for there will come a time when our universe is no longer able to support intelligent life. If any such beings still exist when that time approaches, their only hope for continued survival may be to make the journey into black holes. It is possible that their science will have been developed to such a degree that they can predict what will happen to them when they do. On the other hand, penetrating the secrets of the black hole may turn out to be impossible. Our hypothetical travelers of the future may have no more idea what fate is likely to befall them than we do.

10

THE EXPANDING
UNIVERSE

For more than two thousand years, from the time of the ancient Greeks to the beginning of the twentieth century, Western philosophers and scientists believed that the universe was static and unchanging. It never occurred to them that the cosmos might be evolving, and if such an idea had been suggested, they would have considered it absurd.

Plato and his pupil and successor Aristotle placed the earth at the center of a perfect, incorruptible celestial vault. Heavenly bodies moved either in circles or in paths that were made up of combinations of circles, and they revolved around the earth at constant velocities.

Copernicus, the fifteenth-century Polish astronomer, placed the sun, rather than the earth, at the center of the solar system, but he did nothing to challenge the idea of an immutable cosmos. When Newton formulated the law of gravitation in the seventeenth century, it began to seem even more unlikely that the universe should undergo any fundamental change. In the Newtonian universe, the stars and the planets were subject to unchanging natural law; they seemed destined to follow the same courses for all eternity.

Until 1917, when the young Einstein sat down in an attempt to find mathematical equations that would describe the state of the universe, this ancient outlook had never been questioned. Einstein was surprised, therefore, when he discovered that his mathematics indicated that the universe had to be either expanding or contracting. It was apparently not easy to give up the old ideas. Einstein, who had broken with scientific tradition in so many other ways, was not willing to give up the conviction that the universe was static. Rather than publish his astonishing results, he began to look for a way to "fix up" the equations.

Einstein quickly discovered that in order to get the results he wanted, it was necessary to add in a certain quantity, which he called the *cosmological constant*. The constant represented a force which cancelled out gravitational attraction at large distances. If it existed, such a cosmological force would have to be a very odd one, unlike any others known to physics. Nevertheless, Einstein believed it had to exist. Nothing else could prevent the universe from constantly changing in size.

Years later, Einstein was to remark that the introduction of the cosmological constant had been the greatest blunder of his career, for in 1929 the American astronomer Edwin Hubble presented proof that the universe was expanding. If Einstein had only resisted the urge to fix up his mathematics, he would have been able to predict this result on theoretical grounds years before Hubble's discovery was made.

Before Hubble could show that the universe was expanding, he had to demonstrate that it was much larger than had previously been thought. At the beginning of the twentieth century, many astronomers, perhaps the majority, believed that the Milky Way—that huge disk of stars of which our sun is a part—*was* the universe. They had observed spiral nebulae

with their telescopes, but these were thought to be interstellar clouds of gas. The astronomical instruments of the day
were not powerful enough to resolve these distant galaxies
into individual stars, and since there was no way to measure
their distance, there was no good reason for believing that
they lay outside the Milky Way.

As a graduate student at the University of Chicago, Hubble had already speculated that the spiral nebulae were distant galaxies similar to the Milky Way. However, he had no
evidence to support his ideas. Before he was to have the necessary observational data, six years of work with the new
100-inch telescope on Mount Wilson, in California, was
required.

When, at the end of 1917, George Ellery Hale, director of
the Mount Wilson Observatory, finished the task of grinding
and installing the 100-inch mirror, he invited Hubble to
come to California and join his staff. The United States'
entry into World War I, however, intervened.

When Hubble did come to Mount Wilson in 1919, he immediately began to study the nebulae. It was not an easy
task. In those days, astronomy could be an exhausting business. The site of the telescope could be reached only by an
eight-mile mule trail from Pasadena. Once an astronomer ar-
rived at the observatory, he could look forward to hours of te-
dious work. The best photographic plates then available were
so slow that it took hours, sometimes days, to make an exposure. Sometimes Hubble had to expose the same plate for
several nights in a row, while keeping the telescope pointed
in the proper direction in the sky.

In 1925 Hubble felt that he finally had the evidence he
needed. He announced to the scientific community that he
had found ways to measure the distances of the spiral nebulae, and that they had proved to be hundreds of thousands or
millions of light-years away, far outside our own galaxy. The
fact that they could be seen at such great distances indicated

that they were huge collections of stars, comparable in size to our Milky Way galaxy. The universe had proved to be many times larger than anyone had previously suspected.

Although this discovery would have earned Hubble a permanent place in the history of science, he did not stop there. Instead, he immediately turned his attention to a new problem.

It had been known for some time that the light from the various nebulae was always shifted toward the red end of the spectrum. As every physicist knew, a *red shift* could mean only one thing: these galaxies were moving away from us. Now that he had methods of telling how far away galaxies were, Hubble decided to study this effect. By 1929 he had not only measured the distances to some two dozen galaxies, he had also determined their speed.

The results were astonishing. Not only were the galaxies running away from the Milky Way at enormous velocities, the speed of recession also increased with distance. A galaxy 2 million light-years away moved twice as fast as one at a distance of only 1 million. Galaxies 4 million light-years away moved faster still. There was only one conclusion that could be drawn from this: the universe was expanding.

It appeared as though the galaxies were all trying to fly away from the earth, but this, of course, was only an illusion. In an expanding universe, every galaxy recedes from every other; the expansion as seen from the earth has the same appearance that it would have at any other point in the universe.

This fact is often illustrated by the following analogy. A balloon on which a number of dots have been drawn is blown up. As the balloon expands, each dot will recede from every other. Another analogy, which I prefer, compares the universe to a loaf of raisin bread. As the dough expands (rises), the raisins all move away from each other. The galaxies are like the dots in the first example and like the raisins in the second. Only the galaxies move apart, not the stars within them. Neighboring stars remain approximately the same distance from one another; each galaxy is held together by gravitational attraction.

Hubble found that the speed of recession of a galaxy was proportional to its distance. This fact is known as *Hubble's law*. The simplicity of this mathematical relationship makes it easy to work backward. If the universe is flying apart, then it seems logical that it should initially have been in a very compressed state. A simple calculation should tell us how long ago this compressed state existed. In other words, we should be able to use Hubble's law to determine the age of the universe.

When Hubble performed this calculation, he obtained the result that the expansion began approximately 2 billion years ago. But it soon became apparent that there must be something wrong with this figure. Radioactive dating of rocks from the earth showed that some of them had been formed 3 billion years in the past. Obviously, the earth could not be a billion years older than the universe itself.

The discrepancy was not cleared up until the 1950s, when it was found that some of Hubble's distance measurements had contained a systematic error. He had used certain kinds of variable stars called *Cepheids* as a yardstick, not realizing that there were two different kinds. Using the 200-inch telescope at the Hale Observatory on Mount Palomar, California, Hubble's successor, Walter Baade, was able to show that there were two distinct types of Cepheids. Taking this into account, he recalculated the age of the universe and came up with a figure of 5 billion years.

During the last quarter century, techniques of computing astronomical distances have been refined even further, and the age of the universe has again been revised upward, to a figure of 15 to 20 billion years. These frequent changes do not indicate that there was anything wrong with Hubble's original theory. They simply reflect the difficulties associated with making measurements that are based on observations of the faint light which comes to us from distant galaxies.

When Hubble announced his startling results in 1929, the Belgian priest and astronomer Georges Lemaître had already advanced the theory that in the beginning all of the matter in the universe had been concentrated in a massive "primeval atom," which then exploded, expelling the material from which the galaxies were to form into space.

Although scientists rarely speak of "primeval atoms" today, Lemaître's explanation for the expansion of the universe has, in recent years, come to be almost universally accepted. There seems to be little doubt that the universe was born in an enormous fireball, and that it was the resulting *big bang* explosion that sent matter flying into space.

The big bang theory did not gain immediate acceptance. For years, there were two competing theories of the universe, each with a large number of adherents. Not until 1965 did scientists have any compelling evidence to cause them to favor one theory over the other.

Perhaps there is something about the idea of a static universe that gives it a certain philosophical appeal. Or perhaps that "philosophical appeal" is nothing more than the force of habit. When human beings have believed something for two thousand years, they generally prove unwilling to give up their ideas without a fight.

In 1948 three Cambridge University astronomers, Hermann Bondi, Thomas Gold, and Fred Hoyle, propounded a theory which said that the universe, contrary to all appearances, was not changing. If their *steady state* theory was to be believed, there had never been any big bang. The universe had always existed, these astronomers said, and it had never changed in any fundamental way. In spite of the evidence which showed that the universe was in a state of expansion, the density of matter remained constant. Galaxies had always been and always would be, on the average, the same distance apart.

The steady state theorists did not deny that a state of expansion existed; that was experimental fact. They did suggest, however, that when two galaxies moved far away from one another, then a new galaxy would come into existence between them. There would be just enough new galaxies to compensate for the effects of the expansion. As a result, the universe would always have roughly the same appearance.

Suppose, for example, that two galaxies are 10 million light-years apart. In time (i.e., by around the year 10,000,001, 980, give or take a few billion years), this distance will increase to 20 million light-years. According to the steady state theory, this is just the time required to make a new galaxy. If the new galaxy appears halfway between the two old ones, we will once again have galaxies that are 10 million light-years away from one another. It isn't even necessary to assume that this process makes the universe any bigger. It might be infinite to begin with.

At first glance, such an idea seems extremely implausible. Galaxies do not suddenly pop into existence. Bondi, Gold, and Hoyle had, however, an answer to this objection. In such an enormously long period of time, they said, hydrogen atoms could slowly come into being in intergalactic space. The hydrogen would eventually coalesce into vast clouds of gas, and the mutual gravitational attraction of the gas particles would cause the hydrogen to form pockets that would condense into stars.

Today most people are aware that matter can be turned into energy—in a nuclear reactor, for example, or in the explosion of a nuclear bomb. Some know also that the reverse process can take place—that energy can be transformed into matter. To such people, the steady state theory might seem to be very reasonable.

But Bondi, Gold, and Hoyle were not saying that matter

was created out of energy or out of anything else. They postulated that the intergalactic hydrogen was created out of nothing.

Although this idea of spontaneous creation was unlike any that had ever been suggested before, the steady state theory gained quite a bit of acceptance. For one thing, it was the only reasonable alternative to the big bang. Furthermore, its basic premise was not so odd as it seemed. Although no one has ever observed spontaneous creation, the idea really cannot be disproved. The rate at which matter, according to this theory, would have to be created was so low that it seemed highly unlikely that the process could ever be observed. In a space the size of an average physics laboratory, only one new hydrogen atom would have to be created every thousand years to provide the amount of new matter needed. The universe is so vast that, on the average, it does not contain very much matter to begin with. According to current estimates, if all the matter in galaxies were smeared out evenly through space, there would be only one atom for every 5 or 10 cubic yards.

Some scientists preferred to develop the idea of a big bang universe. At about the same time that the steady state theory was proposed, the American physicists George Gamow, Ralph A. Alpher, and Robert Herman together elaborated on Lemaître's idea of a primeval atom.

Originally, Gamow, Alpher, and Herman said, the universe might have been made up of a dense glob of material consisting of protons, neutrons, electrons, and other subatomic particles. If this assumption were made, Gamow and his colleagues added, it was possible to calculate that within a half hour after the creation, most of the hydrogen and helium in the universe would have been formed and that it would be flying apart in a rapid expansion. Eventually the hydrogen and helium would condense into stars and galaxies, producing the expanding universe that we see today. Since hydrogen and helium are the major constituents of stars, it was not necessary for the big bang theorists to say anything about the formation of heavier elements. As we saw in Chapter 3, these are "cooked" in stellar interiors and spread through space by supernova explosions.

Since discussions of the big bang theory often use such terms as "creation" and "the origin of the universe," it can sometimes seem that we are no longer talking about physics, but are trespassing into the field of theology. Therefore, a word of caution is necessary. When scientists speak of "the origin of the universe," they refer to the beginning of the universe as we know it. They do not mean to imply that nothing existed before a certain point in time—only that they know of no way to extrapolate backward beyond that point.

Scientists can describe the expanding universe in mathematical terms and then work backward. When they do, they reach the conclusion that a big bang probably took place. But if they try to go further back, their equations cease to have any meaning. Certain quantities appear to become infinite, creating impenetrable mathematical barriers. Given our present state of knowledge, there is no way to go any further. It is possible that there may never be. To ask what happened before the big bang is to pose a question that cannot be answered. There may not even be any such thing as "before"; time itself may have come into existence in the initial explosion.

Of course, it is always possible to speculate, as we will see in the following two chapters. It has been suggested, for example, that a whole succession of universes might have existed before ours was created, but scientists who discuss such things come close to mixing metaphysics with science. All that we can be reasonably sure of is that 15 or 20 billion years ago there was an explosion in which the present expanding universe was born.

The big bang theory is well established today. At the time

that it was proposed, however, there were apparently no good reasons for preferring it to the steady state theory of the universe. Some of the evidence seemed to favor the big bang; other experimental facts supported its competitor.

According to the big bang theory, between 23 and 29 per cent of the hydrogen in the universe should have been converted into helium in the primordial fireball. Calculations based on spectroscopic analysis of the light from stars and galaxies confirmed this prediction: the universe was roughly one quarter helium. The evidence was suggestive, but not conclusive. Since the helium could presumably have come into existence in other ways, the steady state theory was not ruled out. All that one could say was that the big bang theory seemed to be consistent with the experimental facts.

Another prediction seemed not to be borne out by experiment. Shortly after the big bang theory had been elaborated, Alpher and Herman had shown that the light from the initial big bang explosion should still be visible. Since it had been traveling through expanding space for so many billions of years, it should have undergone an enormous red shift, but it should still be present in the form of radio waves. A radio wave, like light, is a form of electromagnetic radiation. The only difference between the two is that the wavelengths of radio waves are much longer. Visible light from the stars is often red-shifted into the infrared area, beyond the visible spectrum. Light from the big bang could easily be red-shifted all the way into the radio band.

The big bang theorists realized that these radio waves should be constantly reaching the earth from every direction of space. The reason why they should be everywhere is that the big bang took place everywhere. There was no explosion outward into space—space itself was created in the primeval fireball. There was no such thing as "outside." In fact, if the expanding universe is viewed as an explosion that is still going on, then we are within that explosion. Radiation, there-fore, should reach us from all directions.

Unfortunately, these radio waves had never been observed and thus this theoretical prediction seemed not to be confirmed. To many scientists, this was sufficient reason for favoring the steady state theory, which predicted no *radiation background*.

It has frequently been observed that important scientific discoveries often happen by accident. It should come as no surprise that the radiation background should have finally been discovered by a pair of scientists who were not even looking for it. In fact, since they were not cosmologists, they did not even know that its existence had been predicted. Nevertheless, it was their discovery which led to the demise of the steady state theory and which established the big bang universe in its place.

By 1964 numerous communications satellites were circling the earth. Bell Telephone Laboratories became involved in attempts to solve some of the problems that were associated with their operation, one of which involved the "radio noise," or static, that was always present. If some of the static could be eliminated, then communication by satellite would become easier and more efficient and less powerful radio sig-nals could be used.

Two Bell scientists, Arno Penzias and Robert Wilson, were assigned the task of finding the sources of static in a radio antenna that had been built for communication via the Echo satellites. Penzias and Wilson eliminated as much noise as they could, but the static that remained was more in-tense than it should have been.

Penzias and Wilson carefully checked their equipment, trying to find the source. At one point they thought they had traced the problem to what they described as a "white dielec-tric material" left by some pigeons that had been roosting in the antenna. But even after this was removed, the background static persisted.

The significance of the mysterious radio noise wasn't cleared up until Penzias happened to mention the problem in a phone conversation with astronomer Bernard Burke. It so happened that Burke had recently heard a talk given by the Canadian P. J. E. Peebles, a theoretical physicist at Princeton, in which Peebles had happened to mention that there ought to be a background of radio noise left over from the big bang but that it had not been detected.

Penzias got in touch with Peebles and his collaborators. It soon became apparent that the static that Penzias and Wilson had been hearing was not caused by any defect in their electrical circuits, or by the pigeon droppings, or by anything else having to do with the equipment. What they had been hearing was the universe itself.

It was agreed that Penzias and Wilson should publish their findings in the *Astrophysical Journal* and that the Princeton theorists should submit a companion piece giving the theoretical interpretation. Penzias and Wilson proceeded in the typically cautious scientific manner, titling their paper "A Measurement of Excess Antenna Temperature at 4,080 Mc/s." The theorists explained that this "excess antenna temperature" was the radio background that the big bang theory predicted.

Since the publication of these papers in 1965, more experiments have been performed. The static discovered by Penzias and Wilson, or *cosmic microwave radiation background* as it is now called, seems to have just the form that it should. It has been determined that the background is similar to radiation that would be emitted by a black body at a temperature 2.7 degrees above absolute zero—just what the big bang theory predicts. In 1978 Penzias and Wilson received the Nobel Prize for their work.

We can be fairly certain, then, that the universe began

with a big bang and that it has been expanding ever since. But will this expansion go on forever or will it finally reverse itself, causing the universe to enter a state of contraction?

This is not an easy question to answer. It is fairly obvious that gravity must be causing the expansion to slow down. Gravitational attraction, after all, acts in such a way as to tug backward on the outwardly flying galaxies. The gravitational force may, however, only slow the galaxies down and never cause them to stop. If they fly outward for a long enough time, they will be beyond the range of gravity.

In order to illustrate the uncertainties involved, we might take a look at a quantity which scientists call the *deceleration parameter*. The deceleration parameter is a number, defined by the theory of general relativity, that tells us how rapidly the expansion is decelerating.

At first, everything seems straightforward. It turns out that if the deceleration is greater than one half, the universe will eventually begin to contract. The best experimental value is 1, which is certainly greater than one half. Unfortunately, we can't conclude from this that a state of contraction will eventually be reached, because there is an experimental uncertainty of plus or minus 1; the real value of the parameter could be anywhere between 0 and 2. In astronomy, some quantities cannot be determined with any great accuracy!

There is another way of looking at the problem that is likely to give us more insight into what is going on. The more matter there is in the universe, the more gravitational attraction there will be. This is exactly analogous to the fact that the earth has stronger gravity than the moon because it is bigger. Theoretically, all we have to do is look out into the universe and determine how much matter it contains. We should then be able to calculate whether or not there is enough gravitational attraction to halt the expansion.

But the problem is not that simple. When astronomers examine the sky with telescopes, they can only see matter that emits energy of one kind or another. Most of this is concentrated in galaxies. It is easy to determine that the galaxies contain 1 or 2 per cent of the matter that would be required to give us an eventually contracting universe, but we can only make guesses about the amount of matter that we can't see. This might exist in the form of invisible black holes or as intergalactic dust. No one really knows whether matter needed to produce an eventual contraction—the so-called *missing mass*—is there or not.

When this chapter was being written, it had just been reported that observing equipment on NASA's high-energy astronomical observatory satellite HEAO-1 had detected X-ray emissions from two clusters of galaxies in the constellation Aries. These X-rays seem to indicate the presence of large amounts of intergalactic gas left over from the period of galaxy formation billions of years ago. If similar clouds of gas turn out to be present elsewhere in the universe, it is possible that the missing mass might have been found. While gas isn't very heavy, it can make a significant contribution if there is enough of it, and there is certainly enough room in the universe for there to be a lot.

However, even if more gas is found, the question of expansion or contraction is not likely to be settled for some time to come. Scientific opinion is likely to sway in one direction, then in the other, as different kinds of evidence turn up. All that we can really say with any degree of certainty is this: "Either the universe will go on expanding forever, or it won't."

11

THE DEATH OF THE UNIVERSE

If the universe expands forever, nothing will happen that can interrupt stellar evolution. Sooner or later, all the stars will go out. Some will become black dwarfs, and others will transform themselves into neutron stars or black holes. Black hole "superstars" with masses that are millions or hundreds of millions times that of the sun will form in the centers of galaxies. As time passes, these will grow larger and entire galaxies will be transformed into massive black holes.

As all this takes place, the expansion of the universe will inexorably continue; galaxies will move even farther apart. Eventually, if any intelligent beings still exist, they may look billions of light-years into space and see nothing but what is left of their own galaxies.

Eventually, matter itself—or at least that matter which has not fallen into black holes—may begin to disintegrate. The latest theories concerning the behavior of subnuclear particles appear to indicate that nothing is stable over sufficiently long periods of time. If this is true, all matter will eventually disappear. Some of it will be crushed out of existence in black holes; the rest will simply "evaporate." The proton, previously thought to be one of the few stable particles, may eventually decay. The universe will have become a vacant, heatless waste.

It is unlikely that we will ever reach a point where all physical laws have been discovered. It is probably impossible to know everything that there is to be known about nature. It seems reasonable, therefore, to ask whether there might not be some as yet undiscovered process by which a perpetually expanding universe might regenerate itself and avoid the *heat death* that has been described above.

The answer to this question is that there probably isn't any such process, for there is a law of physics called the *second law of thermodynamics* which tells us that such regeneration would be impossible, because, in any closed system, *entropy* must always increase.

The second law is unique among the laws of physics in that it is believed to apply, without exception, to everything; there are no known exceptions. Unlike other laws of nature, the second law does not deal with this or that phenomenon; it states a principle that all physical processes must obey. In other words, it is completely general.

The second law of thermodynamics was discovered during the nineteenth century by scientists who were trying to explain the flow of heat in steam engines. Only gradually did physicists begin to realize that they had stumbled across something which could have much wider applications. When they did, they made one of the most important advances that physics has ever made.

The second law states that, in any closed system, entropy cannot decrease. Stated this way, the second law sounds like a very esoteric thing indeed. It is not, for entropy can be related to a very simple concept—that of *disequilibrium*.

Without disequilibrium—differences in energy content—no

natural processes could take place. A match could not burn if it did not contain a store of chemical energy to release into a lower-energy environment. Hydroelectric power would be impossible if water could not fall from a high level to a lower one, losing gravitational potential energy in the process. There could be no such thing as a hydrogen bomb if energy was not highly concentrated in the nucleus of the atom.

Any body that one encounters in nature can be said to have a certain energy content. Not all of this energy is, however, available for use. The second law says that it is *differences* in energy content that makes things work. As time goes on, these differences tend to disappear. Things average out. The disequilibrium vanishes. A physicist would express this by saying that "entropy increases."

It is easy to give examples of situations where energy exists but cannot be used. For example, any substance whose temperature is not at absolute zero contains heat energy, but no one has ever designed a ship that can operate by extracting heat from the ocean, and no one ever will. The second law says that a ship which took in ocean water, extracted heat, and left a trail of icebergs behind it would be impossible. It would expend more energy to make the ice than it obtained from the water.

Explanations of the second law frequently invoke such concepts as "disorder" and "information." Such ideas are perfectly valid. It is perfectly possible to equate entropy with disorder or to say that the second law tells us that order gives way to disorder in this universe of ours. It is also possible to say that entropy is the opposite of information. A state of low entropy is one which requires a great deal of information to be described, while a system of high entropy and high disorder can be described much more simply. I think, however, that the concept of disequilibrium makes the meaning of the concept of entropy, and of the second law, intuitively much more obvious.

As the stars burn they radiate energy into space. They are hot, and space is cold (yes, empty space can have a temperature, which is a function of the amount of radiation flowing through it). Planets have temperatures that are somewhere in between. It is the flow of energy which makes physical processes and life possible.

The stars will eventually go out. For a while, enough sources of disequilibrium will remain in the universe for new stars to be formed. But, as entropy increases, this will become more and more difficult. Eventually a point will be reached where it is no longer possible for any new stars to be created. The universe will progress inexorably toward a heat death because the disequilibrium will have disappeared. Finally, entropy will approach a maximum and the universe will die.

For obvious reasons, human beings do not like to contemplate such dismal prospects. At times there have been attempts to find ways to circumvent the second law. Suggestions have been made concerning ways in which sources of negative entropy, or *negentropy*, might be introduced. For if there only are small exceptions to the second law, if there are ways in which the increase of entropy can somehow be halted, then the universe will not inevitably run down; the prospect of a heat death can be avoided.

The discredited steady state theory which was discussed in the last chapter represented one such attempt. Although the authors of the theory did not think in terms of entropy when they put the theory together, a steady state universe would be one in which the entropy increase would be balanced by the creation of new matter. Because the new matter could condense into stars and galaxies, a source of disequilibrium would exist. Such a universe could have existed from an infinite time in the past, and it could exist for an eternity in the future and never be troubled by the second law.

Unfortunately, the evidence seems to indicate that this is not the case. The presence of the cosmic microwave radiation background provides convincing evidence that the universe came into existence at a definite time in the past. The steady state creation of negative entropy has turned out to be an idea that is just a little too farfetched.

It is sometimes said that life itself is a source of negative entropy. This statement is based on the idea that entropy is the opposite of information. Although no one knows how to measure the entropy of a living organism, it is obvious that a lot of information would be required to describe all the processes that take place within it.

Now, if this is true, then a loophole in the second law has been found. Although it is hard to see what relation there might be between the creation of negentropy in living organisms and the fate of the universe, if the second law can be contradicted in this case, there might be reason to expect that it can also be violated in others.

While it is true that entropy can decrease in biological organisms, there is nothing in the second law which disallows this. The second law of thermodynamics says that entropy increases in a closed system. It does not say that entropy cannot decrease in one part of the system while increasing in another. It only makes statements about the total amount.

No organism or group of organisms constitutes a closed system. Life, after all, is something which interacts with an environment. There is every reason to believe that if we do not try to consider the living creatures by themselves but look at the larger closed system consisting of life and environment, we will find that the second law has not been violated. We cannot look at the biosphere of the earth in isolation, for life feeds on the entropy in sunlight. We cannot even neglect the distant stars, which are responsible for the cosmic rays that cause some genetic mutations.

Moreover, it is clear that if we isolate an organism from everything else, its entropy will increase. If we seal it off from its environment, it will die. No one has ever claimed to observe any negentropy in the corpse lying in a sealed coffin.

Many of the laws of physics are approximations. If there is any such thing as the "ultimate nature of reality," we know of no ways to describe it. Approximate laws do allow us to come close enough so that we can gain reasonably accurate ideas as to how the universe works. Now it could conceivably turn out to be the case that the second law of thermodynamics is only approximate also. For all we know, there might be some exceptional cases in which entropy can decrease. However, all attempts so far to find such exceptions have failed, and until there is some evidence to the contrary, it would be best to continue to believe that the second law can be universally applied.

An ever-expanding universe must eventually become a cold, dark relic. Life, however, might disappear only after a protracted struggle. If one or more advanced civilizations still exist when the last of the stars go out, they might be able to go on for quite a long time. Energy disequilibrium appears, after all, in many different forms. By carefully conserving their energy sources, intelligent beings could maintain their civilizations at low but adequate levels. It would not be possible to engage in such wasteful activities as interstellar travel or population growth, and technology and energy use would have to be kept to a minimum. Life could, however, continue for quite a long time, possibly for hundreds of billions of years.

Although the end could be delayed, even such a minimal civilization would have to come to an end. The amount of disequilibrium in the universe is not inexhaustible. Sooner or later an expanding universe must reach a state where the little matter that is left is spread tenuously throughout space, where life is no longer possible, and where everything is of a uniform temperature a fraction of a degree from absolute zero. Unless intelligent beings of the far future find some way to manufacture negative entropy—which, as far as we can tell, is impossible—there will be no escaping the heat death of the universe.

If, on the other hand, the mass density of the universe is above a certain critical value, then we can expect that gravitational attraction will cause the expansion to slow down and eventually stop. When this will happen depends, of course, on exactly how much matter is present. For example, if the mass density is twice the critical value, then the contraction will begin in about 50 billion years. If the density is less, more time will be required; if it is greater, the time scale will be smaller. One can make an analogy between the expansion and the motion of an object thrown upward from the surface of a planet: if the planet is very large, like Jupiter for example, then the object will travel up for only a short period of time before gravity pulls it back; but on a small planet, such as Mercury, it will sail up for quite a long period of time. Since we don't know what the mass density of the universe is, we can't say exactly when the expansion will cease; it might do so in 20 billion years, or in 50 billion, or in 100.

Once the contraction is under way, it will proceed at an ever more rapid rate. As the galaxies come closer together, their gravitational attraction will grow stronger and the process will be accelerated. At first none of this will have any effect on life. When the expansion stops the only observable effect will be that astronomers will perceive blue shifts in the light from the stars. For a while, red and blue shifts will appear together. Since the light from distant galaxies takes longer to reach us, it will still be red-shifted while the light from nearer galaxies will be blue-shifted. When we look at a galaxy that is far away, we are looking at light that was emitted in the distant past. Since the contraction will begin everywhere at the same time, its effects will become apparent in the nearer galaxies first. After enough time has passed, there will of course be blue shifts only.

As the galaxies draw closer together, some of them will begin to collide. Again, this will have little effect on light. As was noted in a previous chapter, the stars in a galaxy are separated by great distances. A galactic collision would cause only a few of them to come close to one another. If any of the planets in the Milky Way still support intelligent life at this time, no one will have very much to worry about, although the astronomers will undoubtedly be able to observe some very spectacular events.

As the contraction nears its final stages, conditions will change dramatically. The entire universe will begin to grow hot, and the night sky will grow progressively brighter. Only part of this light will come from the stars. The cosmic radiation background will still exist, but it will no longer be made up of microwaves. It will have undergone enormous blue shifts which transform it first into infrared radiation and then into visible light.

As the universe contracts, the energy density of both starlight and the cosmic radiation background must increase, for a constant quantity of energy will be confined in less and less space. As a result, the background will be transformed from low-energy radio waves into higher-energy light.

When the universe has contracted to one hundredth of its present size, the night sky will be as bright as the present sky is during the daytime. Then, as the contraction accelerates, it will grow brighter yet. The blue shift will transform light into even more energetic forms of radiation—visible light will be shifted to ultraviolet, and ultraviolet radiation will change into X-rays. The surfaces of planets will grow hot. Soon the radiation will become strong enough to blast molecules apart, and life will no longer be possible.

After all life is gone, the contraction will go on as before. Temperatures will rise to millions of degrees everywhere. The remaining stars and planets will be vaporized and the atoms themselves will be broken apart. Finally, atomic nuclei will be dissociated into their constituent protons and neutrons. Matter as we know it will have ceased to exist; the universe will have entered a state similar to that which existed at its beginning, during the big bang. The only difference will be that there will be an imploding, not an exploding, fireball.

Perhaps it should be emphasized that if intelligent life did somehow manage to survive to this point, it would now be quickly destroyed. It would not be possible for intelligent beings to escape the effects of the implosion by traveling a safe distance from the fireball and observing the destruction from the outside. There will be no such thing as "outside." As we have already pointed out, the universe will not contract in space; space will contract with it. The fireball will be all that is left of space, and of the universe. Everything that exists must necessarily be within it.

It is not possible to follow the contraction to its final stages; we run into the same difficulties that we encounter if we attempt to extrapolate back to the beginning of the big bang. When the temperature and density become high enough, all the known laws of physics break down. It is not possible to say anything about what might happen next.

Long before the contraction reaches this stage, the intelligent beings who inhabit the universe (again, presuming that there are any) will have an agonizing decision to make. When conditions become harsh and life grows difficult, they will have to decide whether they want to attempt to prolong life in this universe a little while longer or to risk instant destruction by traveling into black holes. If they choose the latter, they might find new universes to inhabit.

Of course, one cannot discount the possibility that their physics will be so much more highly developed than ours that they will know exactly what the results of a black-hole journey will be. They may know that anyone who enters a black hole will inevitably be destroyed. On the other hand, they might have found ways to be certain that black holes are gateways to other universes. They might even be able to make choices concerning the kinds of universes they wish to inhabit.

12

THE UNIVERSE REBORN?

Aristotle taught that the heavenly bodies were incorruptible and therefore eternal. The fact that they could not change implied that they must have existed for all time. Creation *ex nihilo* was a concept which found no place in Aristotle's philosophy. Neither did the idea that the universe might eventually be destroyed.

Today we know that the materials of which the universe is built undergo continual change, and we are aware that little or nothing lasts forever. Nevertheless, the idea of a universe which exists from eternity to eternity seems to have as much intuitive appeal today as it did in Aristotle's time. Either the human mind is constructed in such a way that the idea of a universe with a beginning and an end makes us feel uncomfortable, or we find it difficult to break the habits of thinking that have persisted since the time of the ancient Greeks.

It may be that science will never be able to ascertain whether the universe is eternal or whether it exists only between two points in time—some things are beyond the reach of science, and this may be one of them. This, however, does not stop cosmologists from speculating about such matters. Like the rest of us, they seem to like the idea of a universe that will go on forever, and in recent years there have been a number of theories which have attempted to show how this might be possible.

The steady state theory was the first important attempt to posit such a universe, but following the discoveries of Penzias and Wilson of big bang static (see Chapter 10), it seemed that it was necessary to accept the ideas that the universe had a beginning and that it would eventually come to an end, either by contraction, or by heat death if no contraction takes place.

Then scientists began to investigate the possibility that the universe might not be destroyed in an ultimate contraction or collapse. Suppose, they suggested, the matter in the universe was not crushed out of existence as the universe compressed itself into a singularity. Could it not be possible that the universe could somehow bounce back and enter a new state of expansion? If this could happen, there would not be a single big bang, but a series of them. Our universe could have been born out of the collapse of a previous one; in turn, it might give rise to a new universe in the future. Perhaps any given universe could last for only a finite period of time, but why couldn't there be an infinite succession of them?

It must be emphasized that science possesses no evidence whatsoever that such a thing might be possible. However, neither is there any data which would indicate that it is impossible. When one sets up equations that describe the state of the universe, it is only possible to go so far in either direction. When one comes close to either the singularity of the big bang or the singularity in an ultimate collapse, the mathematics suddenly ceases to work, for one has to assume that the density of matter approaches infinity and we know of no way to handle such infinite quantities.

When something lies beyond the boundaries of science, we are free to imagine anything we like. Some scientists have therefore speculated about a variety of possible future universes. They do not demand that these universes must necessarily resemble ours—only that they have laws of physics of some kind and that these laws are consistent.

The simplest kind of future universe would be one that was a direct continuation of our own. It would have the same physical laws and the same physical constants, the same kinds of nuclei and atoms would be formed, and stars and galaxies would presumably be created in the same way. Gravity would behave in the same manner and have the same strength; the speed of light would still be 186,000 miles per second. There might even be the same kinds of intelligent life.

But one thing would be different. If we assume that a new universe is born out of the collapse of the previous one and that all physical laws continue to act in the same way, then entropy must increase from cycle to cycle. Each new universe would begin with the entropy that the previous one possessed when it was destroyed. The second law of thermodynamics would continue to operate during a collapse and the subsequent reexpansion.

This fact has certain consequences. Calculations show that increasing entropy would prevent each cycle from being identical to its predecessor. The oscillations that the universe underwent would grow in amplitude; that is, each universe would expand for a longer time than the previous one. Since the contraction phase must be equal in length to that of expansion, every cycle would be longer than the one before it.

There would be one other important effect. Increasing entropy would ensure that the radiation background was greater in each cycle. This fact has important consequences. Since the radiation background that we now observe is very weak, we can conclude that, if this theory is true, then no very large number of oscillations can have taken place in the past. Calculations have been performed which indicate that, at most, we could be in only the first or second cycle.

This theory, therefore, does not avoid creation at some definite point in time. If we are living in the first cycle, then the big bang was the beginning. If we exist in the second, then the moment of creation is only pushed backward in time. Furthermore, such a universe is really not so very much different from one which expands forever. Since each expansion goes on for a longer time than the one that went before, we will eventually reach a point where expansions are arbitrarily long. We can choose any length of time we like—100 billion years, 1 billion billion, 1 billion billion billion—and there will eventually be an expansion which is longer than that.

There is nothing unreasonable about such a universe. This theory could be an accurate description of the one in which we live. But as long as we are speculating, why not see if we can imagine a universe which does go on forever? If an idea of this sort appeals to us, why not see if it might be possible?

It was suggested long ago that the universe might go through an infinite series of oscillations in which each cycle is of the same length as the last. If such a thing is possible, then there might have been an infinite number of universes in the past, and there may be an infinite number in the future.

Again, our assumption has certain consequences; and again, the second law of thermodynamics is involved. We can assume an infinite number of cycles only if we are willing to admit the possibility that the second law can be violated, that entropy can be destroyed during the collapse of the universe. If it is not destroyed, then we get the universe of lengthening cycles that has just been described.

Some scientists would stop here. They would maintain that giving up the second law would put us on very shaky ground. They would say that the very fact that we have to assume the destruction of entropy means that such a thing would not be possible. Others would not agree. Since we can't calculate what might happen in the collapse anyway, they point out, how do we know that entropy can't be destroyed?

They may have a point. Although we know that entropy increases in our universe, we can't be sure that it will continue to increase during the transition to the next one. It is conceivable that the universe could somehow "reprocess" itself and begin a new phase of expansion at the same low entropy level that it had during the big bang.

However, if one assumes that entropy can be destroyed, one must ask whether the reprocessing might not affect other physical laws also. How do we know that physical constants will remain the same in the new universe? Could not the speed of light be less or greater? Couldn't gravity be stronger or the forces that bind the atomic nucleus together weaker?

According to University of Texas astrophysicist John Archibald Wheeler, physical constants (velocity of light, strength of gravity, and so on) could be different. Furthermore, Wheeler argues, the laws of physics themselves could change in random ways. That is, a new universe might have forces that are unknown in our own, or known forces, such as gravity, could operate according to different laws.

Wheeler's arguments make use of some very abstract mathematical reasoning. He introduces a concept called *superspace*, which possesses a very large, possibly infinite, number of dimensions, and each possible universe is represented by a point in this superspace. Although Wheeler's theory seems to be consistent, there is no way of knowing whether his mathematical treatment has anything to do with reality (whatever that may be). Some scientists think that there exist certain flaws in Wheeler's assumptions. However, since it is all speculation and since there is no experimental data to prove that superspace does not exist, it might be interesting to examine Wheeler's universes more closely and try to see what they would be like.

In the vast majority of cycles, life would not exist. In some of them, the laws of physics would be such that atoms could not exist; in others, no element heavier than hydrogen could form. In some, there would be no stars or galaxies; in others, the nuclear reactions that power the stars would never ignite. Some universes could look very much like our own and yet be lifeless. The laws of chemistry might be such that there would be no such thing as DNA, and nothing else that could act as a carrier of genetic information.

It is not possible to calculate how many of Wheeler's universes would contain life, but it is obvious that they would be a tiny minority. It seems certain that if Wheeler's theory is correct, there are billions or trillions of lifeless cycles for every one that contains living organisms.

Wheeler's theory is certainly an audacious one, but at least it explains why our universe is constructed in such a way as to be so hospitable to life. Most universes are not, the theory says, but there is no one there to perceive them. In the future, there will be numerous lifeless universes, but physical laws and constants will go on changing in a random way until conditions again are such that life can arise.

The superspace theory has one other interesting consequence, one that would be shared by any theory which supposes that the universe goes through an infinite number of cycles. If universes come and go, then sooner or later there must be one very much like our own. This is true whether physical laws change randomly or not. In the former case, it simply takes longer for a universe like ours to happen again, but if infinite time is available, this will inevitably occur.

Some of these universes may be so much like our own that there will be another planet earth, another human race, and possibly even another John Wheeler trying to convince us that such a thing as superspace is possible. Worlds that are almost like ours will be created countless times. There may be one which is like the one we inhabit in every respect except that neither Anchor Press nor a book called *The End of the World* exists. There may be another in which Germany wins World War I, and yet another in which Julius Caesar is not assassinated. And there may be some which are completely indistinguishable from our own.

It is safe to say that there are many scientists who would not accept such ideas, but speculation about the future of our universe is not always meant to be taken all that seriously. The theoretical scientists who engage in it are not trying to describe the nature of reality; rather they are exploring the limits of possibility. When they cannot tell what is true, they try to imagine what might be.

Only when theory is able to suggest experiments that can be performed is it possible to tell what reality is like. So far, no one has found a way to tell whether our universe is the only one that has existed or whether it is a member of an infinite collection. It is just conceivable that there may be some way that we can find out eventually, but no one knows what the experiment that would give us the answer would be like.

And so the speculation continues. Some theorists have tried to go even further than Wheeler and have come up with ideas that are even more audacious. One has suggested that, under certain conditions, time might run backward. Another has questioned whether time might not be cyclical.

We know that, in our expanding universe, entropy increases. But how do we know that it will continue to increase during the contracting phase? The Cornell astronomer Thomas Gold, one of the men who propounded the steady state theory in 1946, has suggested that perhaps it does not. Possibly, Gold postulates, a law of decreasing entropy might hold.

To the lay person there might not seem to be anything very startling about such an idea, but the theory has certain consequences that sound rather fantastic. In Gold's universe, time would run backward during the contracting phase. Rivers would run uphill, rain would rise from the earth to the sky, and energy would fall from space into the sun. People would not grow older, they would become younger; they would begin their lives by rising up out of their graves and die when they entered into their mothers' wombs. This backward universe would eventually end, but in reverse order. The big bang would be the end, not the beginning.

At first, such a theory seems much too bizarre to consider until one realizes that in such a universe our mental processes would also run backward. Since sequences of events and our perception of those events would both be reversed, such a universe would appear to us to be exactly the same as one in which everything ran in the "forward" direction.

In fact, if Gold's theory is correct, then we have no way of telling whether we are living in the "normal," expanding phase or in a time-reversed, contracting universe. The two are exactly equivalent. In Gold's theory the universe has no end —only two beginnings.

Naturally, most scientists do not think that such a situation exists. However, Gold's theory differs from those like Wheeler's in that an experiment can be performed to test it. There is no reason why messages could not be sent from one half of the universe to the other. It is perfectly possible to set up apparatus designed to determine whether any such messages are being received. Of course, the messages would not look like those with which we are familiar. A radio signal coming from the time-reversed half of the universe would not look like a signal to us. Instead, it would take the form of a power drain on radio transmitters in the present.

In 1973 this experiment was performed. The American astronomer R. B. Partridge looked for power drains in a transmitter beamed into outer space and failed to find any. One negative result does not, however, disprove the theory; imagine how surprised we will be if it is repeated in the future, with positive results.

Some scientists have made objections to Gold's ideas on theoretical grounds. It has been suggested, for example, that an intelligent being could presumably survive the moment of maximum expansion (perhaps by sealing itself in a vault) and travel into the time-reversed half of the universe, still living in the "forward" direction. Since the time of this creature would then run in the opposite sense to the time of the half of the universe it entered, its presence might disrupt things to such an extent that the direction of time could be changed over large regions. One would then have a universe in which time ran both ways at once, and causality would be violated.

But who is to say that this is not possible? Physics has great difficulty in explaining why we should experience a subjective time that flows in a certain direction. Most laws of physics are *time symmetric*, in that they have exactly the same form if time is assumed to run in a negative direction. So perhaps the universe is odder than we think. Maybe time reversal in the universe as a whole, or in parts of it, is not something that we should arbitrarily rule out.

P. C. W. Davies, an English mathematician and cosmologist, seeks to avoid the paradoxes that seem to be present in Gold's theory by postulating a universe in which neither intelligent beings nor radio messages can travel across the boundary which separates the "normal" half of the universe from the time-reversed half. Davies' universe is one in which there are two cycles of expansion and contraction. Time runs in the normal direction during both the expanding and contracting phases of the first cycle. The time reversal takes place during the collapse that comes at the end of the contraction. Therefore it is in the second cycle, the one that takes place after the collapse, during which time is reversed.

Since neither living beings nor messages can survive the collapse and reexpansion, communication between the two phases is impossible.

Davies' universe is one in which time is cyclical. Nothing beyond the second cycle is possible, for time is running in the opposite direction there. What we see as its end is really its beginning. A two-cycle universe with time reversal is mathematically equivalent to one in which time runs in a circle. Time is finite, not infinite, yet there is no beginning or end.

It seems that there could be no free will in such a universe, for the future would also be the past and hence would already be determined. But this is not necessarily an objection. No one has ever devised any experiment which can detect the presence of free will. If we decide to reject Davies' theory on these grounds, we must admit that we are appealing to philosophical prejudices, not to observed facts. It is worth mentioning in this connection that behavioral psychologists, such as the American B. F. Skinner, deny the existence of free will without bringing in ideas of time reversal at all.

It might be interesting to note that Davies' universe bears a superficial resemblance to that of the ancient Stoics, who also believed in cyclical time. In the Stoic cosmology, the world was destined to be destroyed by fire and then re-created in exactly the same form. The identical events would take place all over again, until the world perished once more and was again re-created. One only has to replace "destruction by fire" with the more modern notion of collapse of the universe, and Davies' theory and Stoic cosmology become nearly identical.

At least, they do if circular time does imply an endless repetition. Davies maintains that it does not, saying that to draw such a conclusion would be "to invoke the dubious subject of the 'flow' of time." This may be no more than another way of saying that, when one speculates upon such subjects, it is possible to make any assumptions that one wants. Circular time in which things endlessly repeat themselves is no less reasonable than circular time in which they do not. We have no observational evidence that allows us to conclude that either idea is impossible.

If the various theories that we have been discussing seem difficult to swallow, at least one important point has been demonstrated. It is possible to postulate almost any kind of future universe and to describe it in a mathematically consistent way. If science cannot tell us what, if anything, will happen after the universe dies, it has at least shown that almost anything is possible. It is even conceivable that some of these different kinds of universes could exist side by side. There is yet another theory which postulates that all possible universes exist simultaneously, in a manner analogous to the "parallel worlds" of science fiction.

Since the time of the ancient Greeks, scientists and philosophers have been trying to discover the nature of the "real world." But the more we discover, the more nearly impossible such a task seems to be. Now scientists, or at least those who engage in cosmological speculation, seem to be saying that almost anything we are capable of imagining could turn out to be the case. It is enough to make one wonder whether science might not be approaching natural boundaries beyond which nothing is certain. We may obtain evidence that the universe is destined to expand forever, so that a collapse and subsequent reexpansion can be ruled out. If we do not, we will have to accept the conclusion that if the universe can be reborn, this might happen in almost any manner. Time might be circular, or it may be infinite. The cosmos may be constructed in such a way that free will is possible, or it might not. There may even be some sense in which we, or carbon copies of us, will live again.

But there also remains the possibility that death—our deaths, the end of the world, the death of the universe—does finally bring everything to an end.

BIBLIOGRAPHY

I. Books

Anderson, Bernhard W. *Creation Versus Chaos*. New York: Association Press, 1967.

Baade, Walter. *Evolution of Stars and Galaxies*. Cambridge, Mass.: MIT Press, 1975.

Berry, Adrian. *The Iron Sun*. New York: Warner, 1978.

Berry, Michael. *Principles of Cosmology and Gravitation*. London: Cambridge University Press, 1976.

Blacker, Carmen, and Michael Loewe, eds. *Ancient Cosmologies*. London: Allen and Unwin, 1975.

Brandt, John C., and Stephen P. Maran, eds. *The New Astronomy and Space Science Reader*. San Francisco: Freeman, 1977.

Brodine, Virginia. *Radioactive Contamination*. New York: Harcourt Brace Jovanovich, 1975.

Calder, Nigel. *The Key to the Universe*. Harmondsworth, Middlesex: Penguin, 1978.

———. *Violent Universe*. London: Futura, 1975.

Campbell, Joseph. *The Masks of God: Oriental Mythology*. New York: Viking, 1962.

———. *The Masks of God: Occidental Mythology*. New York: Viking, 1964.

Claiborne, Robert. *Climate, Man and History.* New York: Norton, 1970.

Davies, P. C. W. *The Physics of Time Asymmetry.* Berkeley: University of California Press, 1977.

———. *Space and Time in the Modern Universe.* London: Cambridge University Press, 1977.

———. *The Runaway Universe.* New York: Harper & Row, 1978.

Duncan, Ronald, and Miranda Weston-Smith, eds. *The Encyclopedia of Ignorance.* Oxford: Pergamon, 1977.

Eliade, Mircea. *The Myth of the Eternal Return.* Princeton: Princeton University Press, 1954.

Ellison, M. A. *The Sun and Its Influence,* 3d ed. London: Routledge & Kegan Paul, 1968.

Feinberg, Gerald. *What Is the World Made Of?* Garden City, N.Y.: Anchor, 1978.

Frankfort, Henri, et al. *The Intellectual Adventure of Ancient Man.* Chicago: University of Chicago Press, 1946.

Freifelder, David, ed. *Recombinant DNA.* San Francisco: Freeman, 1978.

Gingerich, Owen, ed. *New Frontiers in Astronomy.* San Francisco: Freeman, 1975.

Golden, Frederic. *Quasars, Pulsars, and Black Holes.* New York: Scribner's, 1976.

Goldsmith, Donald. *The Universe.* Menlo Park, Calif.: Benjamin, 1976.

Goodfield, June. *Playing God.* New York: Random House, 1977.

Graves, Robert. *The Greek Myths.* Harmondsworth, Middlesex: Penguin, 1960.

Gribbin, John. *Forecasts, Famines and Freezes.* New York: Pocket Books, 1977.

———. *Our Changing Universe.* New York: Dutton, 1976.

———. *White Holes.* New York: Dutton, 1977.

———, ed. *Climatic Change.* London: Cambridge University Press, 1978.

Grobstein, Clifford. *A Double Image of the Double Helix.* San Francisco: Freeman, 1979.

Guillemin, Victor. *The Story of Quantum Mechanics.* New York: Scribner's, 1968.

Hahm, David E. *The Origins of Stoic Cosmology.* Columbus: Ohio State University Press, 1977.

Hesiod. *Theogony,* in *Hesiod and Theognis,* tr. Dorothea Wender. Harmondsworth, Middlesex: Penguin, 1973.

Hooke, S. H. *Middle Eastern Mythology.* Harmondsworth, Middlesex: Penguin, 1963.

Hoyle, Fred. *Ten Faces of the Universe.* San Francisco: Freeman, 1977.

Inadvertent Climate Modification: Report of the Study of Man's Impact on Climate (SMIC). Cambridge, Mass.: MIT Press, 1971.

Irving, Edward. *Paleomagnetism.* New York: Wiley, 1964.

Kahn, Herman. *On Thermonuclear War,* 2d ed. New York: Free Press, 1969.

Kaufmann, William J., III. *The Cosmic Frontiers of General Relativity.* Boston: Little, Brown, 1977.

Kopal, Zdonek. *The Moon.* Dordrecht, Holland: Reidel, 1969.

Kramer, Samuel Noah, ed. *Mythologies of the Ancient World.* Garden City, N.Y.: Doubleday/Anchor, 1961.

Kuhn, Thomas S. *The Structure of Scientific Revolutions,* 2d ed. Chicago: University of Chicago Press, 1970.

Landsberg, Peter T., and David A. Evans. *Mathematical Cosmology.* Oxford: Clarendon, 1977.

Lear, John. *Recombinant DNA.* New York: Crown, 1978.

Lebovitz, Norman R., William H. Reid, and Peter O. Vandervoort. *Theoretical Principles in Astrophysics and Relativity.* Chicago: University of Chicago Press, 1978.

Marsden, B. G., and A. G. W. Cameron. *The Earth-Moon System.* New York: Plenum, 1966.

Meadows, A. J. *Stellar Evolution.* Oxford: Pergamon Press, 1967.

Misner, Charles W., Kip S. Thorne, and John Archibald Wheeler. *Gravitation.* San Francisco: Freeman, 1973.

Morris, Richard. *Light.* Indianapolis: Bobbs-Merrill, 1979.

Motz, Lloyd. *The Universe.* New York: Scribner's, 1975.

O'Flaherty, Wendy Doniger, tr. *Hindu Myths.* Harmondsworth, Middlesex: Penguin, 1975.

Peebles, P. J. E. *Physical Cosmology.* Princeton: Princeton University Press, 1971.

Ponte, Lowell. *The Cooling.* Englewood Cliffs, N.J.: Prentice-Hall, 1976.

Rogers, Michael. *Biohazard.* New York: Knopf, 1977.

Rowan-Robinson, Michael. *Cosmology.* Oxford: Clarendon, 1977.

Russell, Jeffrey Burton. *The Devil.* Ithaca, N.Y.: Cornell University Press, 1977.

Sagan, Carl. *Broca's Brain.* New York: Random House, 1979.

————, ed. *Communication with Extraterrestrial Intelligence.* Cambridge, Mass.: MIT Press, 1973.

Schwarzbach, Martin. *Climates of the Past.* New York: Van Nostrand, 1963.

Scientific American Editors. *The Solar System.* San Francisco: Freeman, 1975.

Shipman, Harry L. *Black Holes, Quasars and the Universe*. Boston: Houghton Mifflin, 1976.
——. *The Restless Universe*. Boston: Houghton Mifflin, 1978.
Shklovsky, I. S. *Supernovae*. New York: Wiley, 1968.
Singer, S. Fred, ed. *Global Effects of Environmental Pollution*. New York: Springer-Verlag, 1970.
Singh, Jagjit. *Great Ideas and Theories of Modern Cosmology*, 2d rev. ed. New York: Dover, 1970.
Strangway, David W. *History of the Earth's Magnetic Field*. New York: McGraw-Hill, 1970.
Sturluson, Snorri. *The Prose Edda*, tr. Jean I. Young. Philadelphia: Saifer, 1955.
Swihart, Thomas L. *Astrophysics and Stellar Astronomy*. New York: Wiley, 1969.
Taylor, John G. *Black Holes*. New York: Random House, 1973.
Tucker, R. H., et al. *Global Geophysics*. London: English Universities Press, 1970.
Turner, Ron, ed. *Anthology of Slow Death*. Berkeley: Wingbow, 1975.
Turville-Petre, Gabriel. *Myth and Religion of the North*. New York: Holt, 1964.
Verschuur, Gerrit L. *Cosmic Catastrophes*. Reading, Mass.: Addison-Wesley, 1978.
Wald, Robert M. *Space, Time, and Gravity*. Chicago: University of Chicago Press, 1977.
Weinberg, Steven. *The First Three Minutes*. New York: Basic Books, 1977.

II. *Articles*

"Air Samples Reveal New Threat to Ozone." *Science News*, Vol. 114, Sept. 23, 1978, p. 212.
Bahcall, John N., and Raymond Davis, Jr. "Solar Neutrinos: A Scientific Puzzle." *Science*, Vol. 191, Feb. 23, 1976, pp. 264–67.
Bray, J. R. "Pleistocene Volcanism and Glacial Initiation." *Science*, Vol. 197, July 15, 1977, pp. 251–53.
Clark, D. H., W. H. McCrea, and F. R. Stephenson. "Frequency of Nearby Supernovae and Climatic and Biological Catastrophes." *Nature*, Vol. 265, Jan. 27, 1977, pp. 318–19.
Clayton, Donald D., Michael J. Newman, and Raymond J. Talbot, Jr. "Solar Models of Low Neutrino-Counting Rate: The Central Black Hole." *Astrophysical Journal*, Vol. 201, Oct. 15, 1975, pp. 489–93.
Cocke, W. J. "Statistical Time Symmetry and Two-Time Boundary Conditions in Physics and Cosmology." *Physical Review*, Vol. 160, Aug. 25, 1967, pp. 1,165–70.

Cohn, Norman. "Monsters of Chaos." *Horizon,* Vol. 14, Autumn 1972, pp. 42–47.

Cox, Allan. "Geomagnetic Reversals." *Science,* Vol. 163, Jan. 17, 1969, pp. 237–45.

Davies, P. C. W. "Closed Time as an Explanation of the Black Body Background Radiation." *Nature/Physical Science,* Vol. 240, Nov. 6, 1972, pp. 3–5.

———. "How Special Is the Universe?" *Nature,* Vol. 249, May 17, 1974, pp. 208–9.

Davis, Raymond, Jr., and John C. Evans, Jr. "Neutrinos from the Sun." Brookhaven National Laboratory Report No. BNL-22920, Brookhaven, N.Y.

———, Evans, J. C., and B. T. Cleveland. "The Solar Neutrino Problem." Brookhaven National Laboratory Report No. 24629, Brookhaven, N.Y.

Dunn, J. R., et al. "Paleomagnetic Study of a Reversal of the Earth's Magnetic Field." *Science,* Vol. 172, May 21, 1971, pp. 840–45.

"E Pluribus Unum." *Scientific American,* Vol. 240, June 1979, pp. 93–96.

"Earth's Plantlife: Ultraviolet Peril." *Science News,* Vol. 108, Aug. 23 and Aug. 30, 1975, pp. 122–23.

Eberhart, Jonathan. "Of Life and Death and Magnetism." *Science News,* Vol. 110, Mar. 27, 1976, pp. 204–5.

Evans, D. L. and H. J. Freedland. "Variations in the Earth's Orbit: Pacemaker of the Ice Ages?" *Science,* Vol. 198, Nov. 4, 1977, pp. 528–30.

"Following the Trail of a Magnetic Reversal." *Science News,* Vol. 99, May 29, 1971, p. 366.

Green, Louis C. "Supernovae Today." *Sky and Telescope,* Vol. 54, July 1977, pp. 11–14.

Hallam, A. "Mass Extinctions in the Fossil Record." *Nature,* Vol. 251, Oct. 18, 1974, pp. 568–69.

Hartline, Beverly Karplus. "In Search of Solar Neutrinos." *Science,* Vol. 204, Apr. 6, 1979, pp. 42–44.

Hawkes, Nigel. "Smallpox Death in Britain Challenges Presumption of Laboratory Safety." *Science,* Vol. 203, Mar. 2, 1979, pp. 855–56.

Hays, J. D., John Imbrie, and N. J. Shackleton. "Variations in the Earth's Orbit: Pacemaker of the Ice Ages." *Science,* Vol. 194, Dec. 10, 1976, pp. 1,121–32.

Heath, Donald F., Arlin J. Krueger, and Paul J. Crutzen. "Solar Proton Event: Influence on Stratospheric Ozone." *Science,* Vol. 197, Aug. 26, 1977, pp. 886–88.

Kukla, G. J., and R. K. Matthews. "When Will the Present Interglacial End?" *Science,* Vol. 178, Oct. 13, 1972, pp. 190–91.

McCrea, W. H. "Ice Ages and the Galaxy." *Nature,* Vol. 255, July 19, 1975, pp. 607–9.

McElhinny, Michael W. "Geomagnetic Reversals During the Phanerozoic." *Science,* Vol. 172, Apr. 9, 1971, pp. 157–59.

"Ozone Destruction Exceeds Predictions." *Science News,* Vol. 114, Dec. 9, 1978, p. 407.

"The Ozone Layer: The Threat from Aerosol Cans Is Real." *Science,* Vol. 194, Oct. 8, 1976, pp. 170–72.

Panofsky, Hans A. "Earth's Endangered Ozone." *Environment,* Vol. 20, April 1978, pp. 16–20+.

Pathria, R. K. "The Universe as a Black Hole." *Nature,* Vol. 240, Dec. 1, 1972, pp. 298–99.

"Prediction of Ozone Loss Down, and Up." *Science News,* Vol. 111, June 11, 1977, pp. 372–73.

Purrett, Louise. "Magnetic Reversals and Biological Extinctions." *Science News,* Vol. 100, Oct. 30, 1971, pp. 300–1.

Ruderman, M. A. "Possible Consequences of Nearby Supernovae Explosions on Atmospheric Ozone and Terrestrial Life." *Science,* Vol. 184, June 7, 1974, pp. 1079–81.

Russell, Dale, and Wallace Tucker. "Supernovae and the Extinction of the Dinosaurs." *Nature,* Vol. 229, Feb. 19, 1971, pp. 553–54.

Thomsen, Dietrick E. "Supernovas." *Science News,* Vol. 111, Jan. 29, 1977, pp. 76–78.

Trefil, John F. "Missing Particles Cast Doubt on Our Solar Theories." *Smithsonian,* Vol. 8, March 1978, pp. 74–80.

Ulrich, Roger K. "Solar Neutrinos and Variations in the Solar Luminosity." *Science,* Vol. 190, Nov. 14, 1975, pp. 619–24.

Wetherill, George W. "Apollo Objects." *Scientific American,* Vol. 240, March 1979, pp. 54–65.

Whitten, R. C., et al. "Effects of Nearby Supernova Explosions on Atmospheric Ozone." *Nature,* Sept. 30, 1976, pp. 398–99.

INDEX